fantastic rooms

special photography by richard foster

fantastic rooms

how to create 12 decorating styles from around the world

liz wagstaff

Quadrille

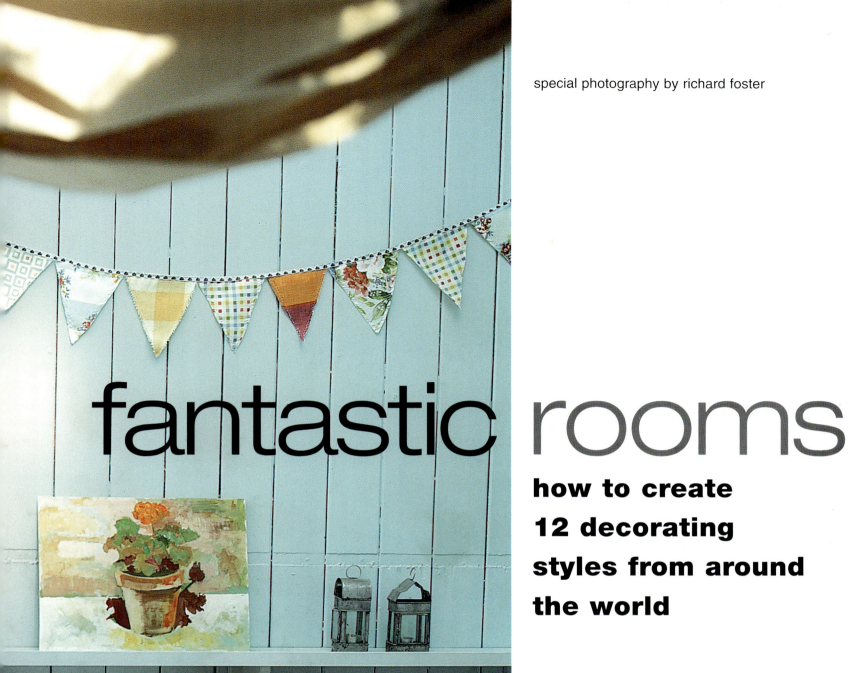

The publisher takes no responsibility for any injury or loss arising from the procedures or materials described in this book. Materials, tools, skills and work areas vary greatly and are the responsibility of the reader. Follow the manufacturers' instructions and take the appropriate safety precautions.

First published in hardback as *Creating a Look* in 1999 by
Quadrille Publishing Limited
Alhambra House
27-31 Charing Cross Road
London WC2H 0LS

First published in paperback in 2001

Copyright © Text Liz Wagstaff 1999
Copyright © Design and layout Quadrille Publishing Ltd 1999
Copyright © Special photography Richard Foster

Art Director **Mary Evans**
Editorial Director **Jane O'Shea**
Art Editor **Rachel Gibson**
Project Editors **Heather Dewhurst** and **Pauline Savage**
Picture research **Nadine Bazar**
Production **Julie Hadingham**

All rights reserved. No part of this book may be reproduced, stored in a retrieval system, or transmitted in any form or by any means, electronic, electrostatic, magnetic tape, mechanical, photocopying, recording or otherwise, without prior permission, in writing, from the publisher.

British Library Cataloguing in Publication Data

A catalogue record for this book is available from the British Library

ISBN 1-902757-73-4

Printed and bound by Dai Nippon

contents

6 Introduction

8 part one the looks

10 The Long Island look

16 The Chinese look

24 The Italian look

30 The Moroccan look

36 The New York loft look

44 The Irish Georgian look

50 The Scottish look

56 The Mexican look

64 The Scandinavian look

70 The Indian look

78 The French look

84 The Greek look

90 part two the projects

92 Decorative Projects

116 Soft Furnishing Projects

132 Construction Projects

150 Templates

156 Stockists and Suppliers   **158** Index   **160** Acknowledgments

introduction

I love travelling, but going abroad has always held danger for me, not from the animals or natives but from the wealth of wonderful ideas for decoration that I bring home, and the passionate desire I have to reproduce these ideas in my own and other people's homes! Memories of holidays are precious and it is only natural to try to relive some of the magic by transforming a room in your home into a permanent reminder of a much loved trip. Simply by changing the colour of a room you can instantly evoke another country. For example, using intense whites and blues can evoke the bright sun and clear blue seas of Greece, while sultry ochres and rich earthy tones can conjure up the souks and Berber markets of Morocco. By adding suitable furnishings and accessories, you can then be transported back to your favourite holiday destination! *Creating a Look* is a trip around the world via interior decoration and *en route* it will provide the key to successfully recreating these looks in your home.

I know from experience how embarking on this type of decoration is not always straightforward, with the paints and other decorative materials available lacking that certain authenticity. However, with the vast leaps in paint technology and the increased interest in ethnic decoration it is now far easier to achieve stunning results than ever before. In planning this book, I found it difficult to limit my choice to just twelve looks, each with so much to offer. However, these are my favourites and I felt these would translate more easily than others. These looks are all easy to live with and each suits the particular rooms given. Having said that, there is no reason why one look could not be adapted to decorate a different room from the example shown.

The elegance and richness of Indian decoration made this one of the first choices. I love the hot spicy colours that are used so much in the homes, not just on the walls and fabrics but in Indian cooking too. Another style that is full of magical colours is that of Morocco. A walk through the souk offers vibrant primary colours in the tiles and fabrics, while deep ochres and mud tones adorn the rough ancient walls; my favourite Moroccan colour is the deep ultramarine blue that is used in so much of the interior decoration.

I looked a little closer to home for the stunning Irish Georgian look, whose dark brooding effect smacks of peat fires and candlelight. This simple elegant style is easy to achieve and also inexpensive through the use of cunning tricks that make a period style affordable in any home. Next, I was inspired by the tweeds and tartans of the Scottish Highlands to adorn a homely country study full of memorabilia and cosy textures.

America was the next stop for two very different looks, the clean modern style of the New York loft where industrial furniture mixes with bright bold colours, and the sunbleached tones of the Long Island beach house, where faded florals, shells and driftwood are used to great effect. Then we drop down to Mexico for a kitchen with a vivid mix of colour that sums up the energy and resonance of the people. To create a sleek and sophisticated living room, I chose the Orient for inspiration; this room combines silks and lacquers with natural bamboo.

Two simple yet stylish looks were inspired by colour: the cool blues and deep reds of Sweden for a relaxing bedroom, and the clean whites and strong blues of the Aegean for a minimalist bathroom. The Italian look is one I have loved for a long time; its crumbling elegance and classical overtones have always held magic for me and it is an ideal look to recreate. In this room, inexpensive plaster statues and plastic urns were transformed into priceless antiques with just a lick of paint! The Parisian boudoir, too, had long been a favourite of mine; I gave it a modern twist to create a cool, feminine interior in which to relax, pamper and indulge oneself.

Creating a Look is divided into two parts. Part One contains the interpretation of these twelve looks, showing how they are inspired by the landscape, history and culture of the particular countries, and how they are created by the use of paint, fabric, furnishings and decorative accessories. You may choose to recreate the whole effect or just adapt some of the style ideas for your home. The instructions for the projects featured in these looks are contained in Part Two of the book. Each project contains a list of materials required and the instructions are accompanied by photographs and diagrams. Templates are also included to enable readers to reproduce designs exactly. Finally, a detailed list of suppliers – both retail and mail order – makes sourcing equipment an easy task.

I hope you enjoy your trip around the world through this book and that you are inspired to have a go at redecorating your home in one of the looks shown.

Liz Wagstaff

the

part one

looks

The Long Island look developed naturally from its surroundings of sunshine and sea, when early seafaring whalers and lobstermen constructed simple clapboard huts for shelter along the sea front. Then, when New Yorkers began to look to the seashore for vacations, the basic fisherman's hut became a rustic summer **beach house**: the wooden floors and walls were painted in light pastel colours, while faded florals and handmade quilts softened the interiors. With its informal feel and nostalgia for summers gone by, the Long Island look is ideal for all ages and tastes.

Above: Dappled sunlight filters through the window giving the day room an underwater feel. The simple plate shelf (page 133) is perfect for displaying treasures collected on seaside holidays, while colourful bunting (page 130) continues the nautical theme.

A day room filled with morning light was the ideal setting for the beach house style. Soft and comfortable, yet airy and stylish, it soon became the perfect place in which to relax, surrounded by driftwood and shells, and dreaming of seaside holidays past.

Above: A cigarette card featuring physical exercises makes an ideal sporting print when blown up and colour copied. A wood-washed coral tone for the frames gives a soft, sun-bleached look. Cut flowers displayed simply in glass bottles add to the natural effect by bringing the outside in.

beach house

Above: This large sturdy cupboard was dry-brushed to suggest years of bleaching by the sun and salt winds. It also makes an ideal place to hang strings of shells (page 114), which tinkle like windchimes when they catch the sea breeze.

Retaining the abundant morning sunlight in this tiny space was the main priority, so I chose a colour palette of aqua, pinks and other pastels to reflect as much of it around the room as possible. The tongued-and-grooved walls and large cupboard were painted in the light aqua colour of sunshine skies. Simply made from MDF and finished pine, the plate shelf which runs around the room was painted in the same shade so that it would blend seamlessly into the walls. It makes an ideal display area for seaside memorabilia, such as toy boats, favourite shells and old postcards.

The wooden floor was covered first with a coat of white emulsion, then with 25cm (10in) bands of blue and coral painted with random brushstrokes. The addition of a dry-brushed layer of white over the top suggests a bleached and aged look without the shabbiness. It almost resembles a huge beach towel left out in the sun to dry.

Left: A day bed on castors (page 148) is a comfortable and practical addition to the room. When the canvas blind (page 125) is hoisted, it looks like a clipper leaving for the ocean. When fully unfurled, it diffuses the strong sunlight and billows in the breeze.

Right: Floral and gingham bunting cushions (page 118) are typical of the beach house look. Just imagine lying back with a good book or dozing beneath a sunhat as the sea breaks on the shore outside.

Above: Shells and driftwood drilled through to take the rope work well as an improvised toggle for holding up the sail blind (page 125).

Right: A metal spectator's chair retrieved from a tennis club has been given a new lease of life. Painted and dressed in a contemporary manner, it fits in well with the other sporting details.

A day bed made from finished pine and thick plywood proved a great spot for reading or just taking in the surroundings. Its thick foam mattress upholstered with checked fabric and a backrest of cushions covered in gingham and faded florals reflects the American quilting tradition without introducing too much cottage chinz. Offcuts of the same material were used to make bunting, a fun and pretty nautical addition.

Crisp billowing canvas hung from a woodwashed curtain pole was another nod to the maritime feel. In addition to all the reminders of the seaside, I decided to introduce a sporting theme. An old metal tennis club chair was given a facelift with a coat of soft pink paint and a floral foam cushion attached to the frame with ties. Physical fitness prints enlarged and colour-copied from cigarette cards were mounted in simple colourwashed frames, bringing this look right up to date.

The Chinese look combines the influence of imperial China, with its opulent architectural style, intricate carvings and rich and glorious colours, with the spiritual calm of the ancient Buddhist religion. When these influences are adapted to a metropolitan setting, the look is the ultimate in sleekness. In this **chinese living room**, natural parchment colours set the scene, spiced up with red, black and gold for a hint of sensuousness. Smooth surfaces shine with lacquer, while sumptuous silks add luxury and style.

chinese living room

Left: This glossy lacquered coffee table has been given an authentic Chinese look with an added bamboo magazine shelf (page 137), making it ideal for takeaways.

Left: Natural objects such as pebbles work well with the highly polished finish of lacquer. Try playing with a variety of textures when creating this style.

Below: A lacquered and découpaged screen adorned with writhing dragons (page 103) makes a stunning decorative barrier. The black leather-covered cube can be used as a table or as extra seating.

The lofty proportions of this room with its straight lines and plain features made it ideal for a touch of the Orient. By mixing natural colours and textures together with luxurious soft silks and opulent velvets, the room soon took on the extravagant yet sophisticated look of the East.

Left: Opulent silks and simple rattan provide alternative aspects of Chinese decoration: the stylish luxury of the city and the natural textures of the countryside.

Before any decoration could take place, some construction work needed to be done. A small cupboard next to the fireplace was removed and shelving was built in the alcoves on either side of it.

Then the window frame was painted with a cream acrylic eggshell, while the rest of the woodwork was painted black. The walls were given two coats of a parchment colour emulsion before being colourwashed with a white glaze to give a broken colour effect, allowing some of the base coat to show through. This was then softened to remove some of the brushstrokes, and an antiquing wax was rubbed in to age and seal the surface, giving a stone-like sheen. The shelves in the alcoves were given the same decorative parchment technique and then concealed with doors constructed from framing moulding with silk panels stretched within them.

A natural flooring was chosen for the room, and a black jute-bound rug in a deeper gold tone was laid on top to break up the effect. A low day bed was constructed from thick MDF with fretsawed designs inset in its sides; this was upholstered with foam cushions covered in a luxurious red velvet. Black leather cubes offered further seating. More storage was provided with a simple cube unit which was painted with two coats of black acrylic gloss. Doors were fitted to the front, and decorative round brass discs were attached to

Above: Sumptuous silks in the form of heavy interlined drapes sit well with simple rattan and bamboo. The screen is a simple construction using bamboo poles and fencing (page 143). The drapes and fabric-covered pelmet add dramatic elegance to the muslin blind which is held in place by cotton ties (pages 122-3).

Right: Framing mouldings make ideal frames for the alcove shelves, which are screened from the room by silk-covered panels (page 140). These hide all the living room essentials of stereo, compact discs and videos in a stylish way.

Above: A simple cube unit is given the oriental touch with the addition of doors decorated with brass discs (page 134). The mandarin-style pediment with its fretsawed design makes a bold statement. This unit provides ideal storage and display for a mix of practical and decorative items.

them. The unit was surmounted by a mandarin-style pediment with a fretsawed design in the centre, echoing the circular shapes in the sides of the day bed.

A simple flat-pack table was given extra style with the addition of a bamboo magazine rack. The table was given a lacquer finish, then coated with tinted wood varnish. Finishing touches were added with the application of simple handpainted designs in black and gold.

The same lacquer effect was given to a mandarin-style screen decorated with writhing découpaged dragons. A simpler screen was constructed from a frame of bamboo, backed with bamboo fencing, and bound together with black cord. Bamboo was also used to make Chinese-style standard lamps; lengths of thick bamboo were screwed together to conceal the light lead and fittings, and coloured lanterns were hung from the tops to give lovely soft pools of light.

Adding to the feel of luxury in the room, the sumptuous window drapes were made from parchment-coloured silk bound with a deep edging of black Chinese silk; these were then attached to a wide fabric-covered pelmet. A simple muslin blind secured by long ties completed the window treatment. Adding to the soft furnishings, a variety of cushions were made from gaudily coloured silks both patterned and plain, and backed with deep red velvet. Banners were also made by edging a red patterned silk with a plain black silk.

The Italian look has many facets, whether it is the elegant columns of ancient Rome, the sumptuous Renaissance palaces, the magical classical villas deep in the countryside, or the chic modern residences of Milan. In the **tuscan day room**, architectural elements play an important role, with grand arches and pillars being the dominant features. Faded terracottas, dirty creams and the bold blues of frescoes are typical of the bleached shades found on bare plaster walls, while marble, stone and terracotta combine effortlessly with more sophisticated mosaic and wrought iron.

Right: Pompeii was the influence for this *trompe-l'oeil* arch (page 98), its colours complementing the wall finish. Simple wrought iron trestles with planking make a strong stylish side table (page 135) with plenty of room for displaying inexpensive plaster objects and more obscure collectables, like the beautiful ostrich eggs.

tuscan day room

The scale of this interior, with its large windows and cavernous fireplace, made it perfect for transforming into a Tuscan living room. Frescoes and aged plaster provided the backdrop within which the beautiful shapes and colours of Italian style could be displayed.

Two coats of white emulsion were painted on the walls, and then a pink plaster glaze was applied over the top using a broken colour technique; the brushmarks were softened to give a fresco effect. A *trompe-l'oeil* arch was painted on each side of the fireplace in a mix of techniques using complementary tones. This design implemented both classical and Pompeiian looks.

Wrought iron trestles were used to provide table space; the tabletops were made from rough sawn wood tinted with an antique wax, then limed for a sunbleached look. Two mock columns were fashioned from papier mâché and wood and given a soft neutral sandstone effect; these provided ideal display

Left: A simple throw was made from linen union; excess fabric was drawn up and secured with a gladiatorial tab (page 127). The fake fur throws and sumptuous cushions are the ideal warmers in this cool interior. The large plastic urn was given a terracotta finish (page 113), a technique which can be used to adapt a variety of inexpensive objects.

Right: This *trompe-l'oeil* urn (page 113) provides an unusual way to hide the rather cold black expanse of a fireplace. Place real urns around the screen for a humorous effect.

THE ITALIAN LOOK

Above: This day bed propped with fringed cushions (page 120) is the ideal place for relaxation and dreaming. The papier mâché columns (page 114) make perfect display places for urns and a wonderful clam shell. Try to make big bold statements when dressing a room like this.

Left: This novel idea hides away all your compact discs. A flat-pack CD rack was given a curved ply door to echo a pillar (page 147), then painted with the same finish as the wall.

space for pots and statues. A large plastic urn was decorated with a terracotta paint effect; an equally large plinth was decorated in the same way, as were several varying sizes of urn and pot. Urns and plaster items are remarkably cheap to buy and equally as inexpensive to decorate.

Two plain CD towers were given curved doors made from skin ply and MDF to echo the shape of a pillar; these cleverly disguised today's living room paraphernalia. The towers were decorated using the same finish as on the walls, so as to blend in.

To hide the fireplace, an urn-shaped screen was made from MDF and given a *trompe-l'oeil* effect. When placed among real urns, it made a fun feature. Two canvas floorcloths were made to soften the wooden floor; these were painted in a mock mosaic effect, then softly sanded back.

After all the construction and painting work, it was time to consider soft furnishings. Two tired settees were transformed with inexpensive linen union, a simple solution with classical style. The

Right: A Roman soldier's skirt was the inspiration for the tabs on these simple banner-style curtains (page 123); cool linen union was used as an inexpensive fabric to cover a wide area. The suede-covered buttons provided a finishing touch.

Below: A painted canvas floorcloth (page 99) provides a cheap way to cover a large area. Here it is painted in the same fashion as the walls and a mock mosaic pattern applied with a large flat brush.

Below: These plaster architectural details are easy to find and very cheap; when sealed they can be decorated in a variety of ways. This corbel was given the aged plaster wall finish (page 93) so that it looks like part of the wall.

suede-covered buttons and tabs add to the natural textures and produce a gladiatorial effect. Fake fur cushions and throws added an effect of luxury. An Indian day bed was also covered in linen union, and complemented with cushions covered in classical-style fabric with a deep red fringe. The same fabric was also used to make a new shade for a standard lamp.

To decorate the windows, a simple curtain pole was made from copper piping, then aged using gold patination fluids; shop-bought finials provided the finishing touch. Simple banner-style drapes with tabs echo the simplicity of the soft furnishings, the suede-covered buttons again adding a strong gladiatorial look.

Two contemporary wall lights were retained but were given new parchment shades. Plaster uplighters were bought for the remaining two walls; these were decorated using the same wall effect, and gilt cream was added for extra glamour. Other accessories included inexpensive plaster ornaments and contemporary stone-effect vases.

The Moroccan look draws on a wide range of influences, from the sumptuous tented palaces of the nomadic peoples and the heady spice-filled souks, to the exquisite mosaic decoration of religious temples. The main essence of the Moroccan look is colour – the many shades of sun-baked earth and aromatic spices. A cosy **moorish den** can easily be achieved by using characteristic low seating, intense colours and Moroccan fabrics for tenting. If you add candlelight and incense, you could almost be transported to a Berber tent far away in the desert.

moorish den

Right: A tiny mosaic-topped table and tea glasses are some of the accessories widely available for recreating the Moroccan style.

Above: An assortment of lanterns and candles set the mood of a Moorish den and flicker softly against the stencilled walls (page 97).

For this unusual-shaped room at the top of a house, I recreated the cosy intimate feel of a Moorish den with plenty of atmosphere and intense colours, making it the perfect place for a teenager's hideout.

The deep blue so often seen in Morocco was the starting place for the walls, but before this colour could be painted, the woodchip paper had to go and the bare plaster walls beneath sealed. A line was marked 1m (1¼yd) from the floor and the walls were then painted ultramarine above the line and cream below. A pale pink colourwash was dry-brushed over the blue to produce a bleached effect.

For an extra theatrical feel, an interlocking tile design using blocks of stars and crosses was stencilled on the lower walls in green and orange paint. An coat of antique pine wax was then brushed over the top to age the mosaic. The hardboard floor was painted in the same deep blue as the walls and a red star was added in the centre. This was then coated with clear acrylic floor varnish for durability.

Now for the furniture. An existing cupboard was given a touch of the kasbah with decorative fretwork and studs. The doors

Above: Galvanized lanterns hang from the tent edging (page 146) which is adorned with stencilled stars and antiqued copper studs for a softly aged look.

Above: The mosaic tile-effect wall (page 97) and low seating (page 148) all add to the look of the den. Inexpensive paper star lanterns were placed over standard and table lamps for a twinkling light effect, while the canvas blind and tented ceiling (page 146) complete the look.

were painted deep blue and the framework was then dry-brushed with a coat of dark brown paint. A decorative pelmet was made to sit above the doors. Low adaptable seating was constructed from MDF and given a desert feel with a sandstone paint effect. The seats were made from 10cm (4in) thick foam covered in bright cotton. Adding to the den effect, an ingenious table was made using an old decorative curtain pole and a piece of MDF. This was then painted in the same ultramarine blue and decorated with copper roofing clouts.

The dark mood of the room was drawn on for the tent effect which hid any imperfections in the existing room and gave it its final dramatic touch. The leading edge of the tent was hidden by a castellated border stencilled with stars. A tentflap-style blind was attached to the window frame using eyelets and hooks and then stencilled with stars to match the tent.

Colourful floor cushions were scattered over the floor as decorative accessories, and paper star lanterns were attached to floorstanding lights for stunning sidelights. Lanterns and candles, together with a mosaic-topped tea table, completed the look. This type of room is easy to fill with old and new objects; tea glasses, lanterns, kilims and Christmas baubles all add simple yet decorative touches and are all widely available.

Left: This cupboard is surmounted by a minaret-shaped pelmet (page 141) which has been painted blue, then dry-brushed in a warm chocolate brown and finally adorned with copper roofing clouts.

Below: These old cupboard doors were replaced with decorative fretwork (page 147) and decorated with battens and studs while bright cotton fabric is hung behind the doors for added colour.

Left: This little table (page 136) was constructed from MDF and an old curtain pole, then painted and decorated in the intense way so indicative of Moroccan style.

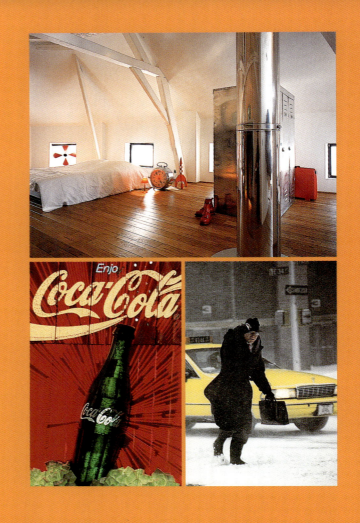

The New York loft look is the ultimate in minimalist chic and ergonomic style. Architectural elements play an important part in creating the crisp lines and hard edges of this distinctive open-plan style, and metal pillars and iron girders are dominant features. In a **new york loft**, brickwork is exposed and often unpainted, providing the perfect backdrop to works of art. This look is for those people who seek an easy-to-maintain yet stylish interior – fussy frills and lacy edges are definitely out.

newyorkloft

With its white walls, tall ceilings and large windows, this room soon took on the feel of a New York loft. All it needed was some bold colours, some industrial scaffolding and a few carefully chosen pieces of furniture and accessories.

Below: The reinforced wired glass of the tabletop (page 137) adds to the industrial feel of the space. The table was constructed by attaching the top to a metal palette painted with hammered metal-effect paint.

Right: A line of polaroid portraits of friends decorates the red wall in the living area. Old clothes pegs attach the pictures to a piece of string that spans the wall.

The starting point was to paint the cleared loft a bright titanium white, to unify the space and make it seem even larger. Next, the floor was treated to lino tiles, which are inexpensive to buy, easy to install and practical for every area of the home.

With the basics catered for, specific zones needed to be created within the larger space, to allow for different activities. To keep the feeling of space while providing some privacy we made a room divider by stringing a canvas screen between two builder's props. The gaps left at top and bottom ensured that light can still travel from one area to another, so there are no dark corners.

The right-hand side of the room became the bedroom area. In keeping with the industrial feel of the loft, we made a bedhead from scaffolding and chose office filing cabinets for use as bedside tables. With no built-in cupboards, a free-standing clothes rail from a commercial supplier provided essential hanging space while shielding the bedroom from the rest of the loft.

Large spaces call for large amounts of furniture which can be very expensive, so some pieces of furniture here are

Left: Quirky vintage furniture gives the loft a certain individuality. The orange conference chairs were picked up from a local second-hand shop. The artwork takes little artistic flair to create (page 110) and is painted in ordinary matt emulsion.

Below: The large white space is punctuated with furniture and accessories in a vibrant red, orange and metallic green. Furniture on castors, such as this low table (page 137), can easily be moved around.

Left: A canvas screen strung between two builder's props (page 143) helps create a room within a room, defining the living and bedroom areas. The canvas does not quite reach to the ceiling or the floor, which preserves a feeling of space and light.

homemade and others are second-hand. At the foot of the bed stands a felt upholstered foam cube for use either as seating or as a table, while a photographer's lightbox makes a novel bedside light.

To save on the expense of covering the large windows with curtains, a cheap but beautiful papery lining was simply fixed to the window frame for an unusual window treatment. These translucent 'curtains' could stay closed all day as they diffuse the light beautifully while still providing a degree of privacy.

Below: A free-standing clothes rail from a shop fittings supplier provides precious storage and acts almost as a second screen, giving the bedroom relative privacy from the rest of the loft. The scaffolding bedhead (page 138) adds to the industrial feel.

The left-hand side of the room became the living area. A single wall painted hot red and a thick rug define the space. A sofa and two vintage chairs flank a low-level coffee table, made from a found metal crate, to make an intimate seating area.

The large white wall above the bed called for overscale art. To avoid gallery prices, a black and white photograph was enlarged to A1 size and mounted on foamboard. Dynamic colour was added with large canvases painted with alternate stripes of red and orange emulsion. Finally, a string of polaroid portraits of friends added a quirky touch.

Below: Two builder's props make a practical frame for a canvas screen (page 143). A length of rope run through an eyelet secures the canvas to the props. The extra width of the canvas means that no sewing skills are required.

Left: Accessorize with colourful candles in bold shapes to continue the decorative theme.

THE NEW YORK LOFT LOOK

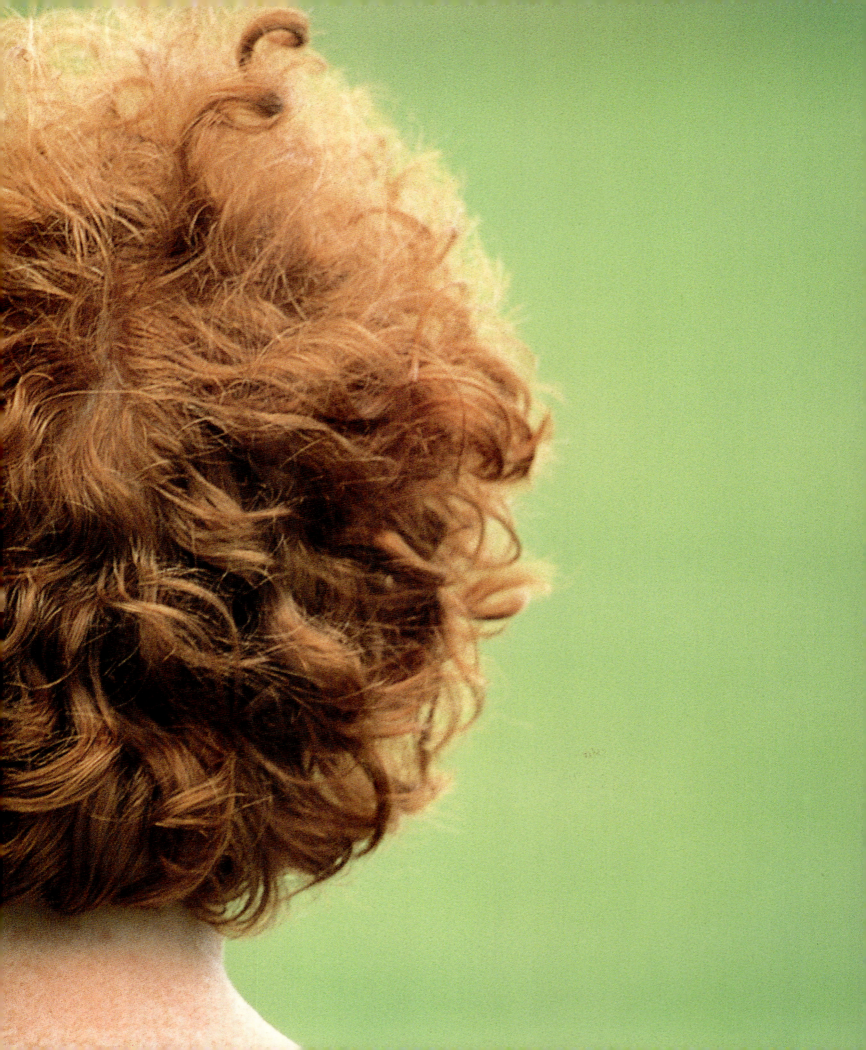

The Irish Georgian look is a period look encompassing both comfort and practicality. An eclectic mix of old and more contemporary styles of furniture and accessories works best and adds to the informal atmosphere created by this look. Textured fabric throws and cushions soften the **georgian parlour** and make it more inviting – choose from deep moody colours or more vibrant ones from the Georgian palette. However you decide to interpret this relaxed look, it will give a sense of history to your home and cannot help but look well lived in.

Left: Make your own silhouettes (page 101) of friends for a personalized touch. You can even leave people's glasses on to create a fun contemporary look!

For this timber-clad interior I recreated the stylish yet unfussy charm of an Irish Georgian parlour. The informal style, with its hints of grandeur, is ripe for modern interpretation, as period pieces sit well with modern furniture and decorative objects.

georgian parlour

Right: A Louis XIV reproduction chair shows how you can interpret a style successfully without adhering strictly to period items. The characters on the upholstery link it in a cheeky way to the 18th century. A herbed cushion, decorated subtly with silhouettes in voile pockets (page 120), adds a feminine touch to this otherwise masculine interior.

The room was designed like a modest 18th century farmhouse to suit its rural setting, sparsely decorated with a few practical but elegant essentials. The lack of much natural light was very atmospheric but it did mean that I had to choose a lighter colour for the walls than is typical of the period – a dirty ochre – to prevent the room from becoming oppressive. Chosen from a modern Georgian palette, it added warmth and cosiness.

The wood-tiled floor was given special treatment with a painted 'rug' in rich green. Stencilled acorns and leaves – a design inspired by the frame of the mirror in the room – formed a colourful border. A tinted wood varnish was applied over the area, not only to protect the paintwork but also to give the floor an aged effect.

The modern tiled fireplace at first seemed difficult to adapt to the Irish Georgian but it is surprising what a lick of paint can do. A deep green colour to match the painted rug was dry-brushed with antique pine woodstain to simulate the residue that can build up in a fireplace. The surround was given extra dimension by the addition of a dramatic overmantel made from MDF. The routed edges of the structure give a period feel while its simple shape gives a nod towards modern minimalism. The ebonized effect was

Right: The ebonized table and chair (page 135) typify the simple, uncluttered Irish Georgian look. A hand-tinted engraving (page 101) and quirky images on the tablecloth (page 108) lend the scene a certain impish charm.

simulated by using blackboard paint buffed up with a cloth to add sheen, which has the bonus of making it a hardwearing heat- and waterproof surface. The kitchen table, chairs, picture frames and curtain pole were also given this treatment.

Now for the detail. For a novel effect, the tablecloth and upholstered chairs were decorated with black and white engravings, which were transferred on to cream duck

Left: The vast overmantel (page 135) over the painted fireplace dominates the room, adding to its moody atmosphere, but the toby jugs and fun silhouettes are a more lighthearted touch. The simple bench and piles of chopped logs are a reminder of the rustic origins of this look.

Far left: This small side unit was a new piece, given period-style legs and a hand-tinted engraving for a tabletop. An old fish slice bent with pliers makes an unusual drawer handle.

Right: Painting a rug is an easy way to disguise a wooden floor with uneven coloration, while keeping the room simple and practical. The acorn-and-leaf border was inspired by the period-style mirror.

canvas with image transfer solution. Period prints or even modern reproductions can be expensive to buy but you can easily make your own using photocopies of images, hand-tinted and aged for a period feel. For the finishing touches, silhouettes were copied from copyright-free sources and mounted in both modern and old-style picture frames, a surprisingly decorative effect that is easy to accomplish.

Right: This cheerful character taken from a copyright-free source book was one of many used to adorn this simple cream tablecloth (page 108).

Above: The eclectic styles of the ebonized chairs (page 135) adds to the ease and charm of the dining room. Modern scented candles placed simply on the floor show how effective it can be to combine old and new styles.

THE IRISH GEORGIAN LOOK **49**

The Scottish look has been strongly influenced by Scotland's rugged terrain and harsh climate, and warmth and comfort are the main criteria. Tartan and tweed, with their lovely texture and beautiful natural hues, are a major component of the **scottish study**. Panelled walls also feature strongly, along with sporting prints and hunting trophies. With its combination of soft textures and natural colours, the Scottish look is an ideal decorating scheme for a study, library or sitting room.

Below: This comfortable velvet-covered chair sits well with the cherry tone of the modern floor rug; the mix of textures and colours creates a cosy, relaxing spot by the fire.

scottish study

The informal charm of this room made it ideal for transforming into a welcoming retreat. Inspired by the colours and textures of the Highlands, the room soon began to convey the atmosphere of a Scottish study.

Left: Pots of heather and other fresh or dried countryside flowers add softness and charm to the room, while their colour echoes the glories of the Highlands.

Left: An appealing combination of checks and tartans in different colours can be seen in the screen (page 128), throws and blankets. These work well with the collection box which also contains its own mix of textures.

Below: A range of appliqué techniques and heavy blanket stitch were used to make this lovely pictorial wall-hanging (page 130), which proved to be an ideal way of using up fabric scraps and exploring a mixture of textures. The transferred images were handcoloured to create a look of aged engravings.

To establish a relaxing air with the feel of the countryside, I chose a leafy green colour scheme for the walls: a light fresh green for the area above the dado rail and on the ceiling, and a deeper leafy green beneath the rail. A stencilled *trompe-l'oeil* panelling was added to the walls beneath the dado rail to give the room a more architectural feel. The walls were then given a light colourwash to age and soften them.

In keeping with the feel of the room, a standard flatpack MDF bookcase was given extra grandeur by the addition of skirting board to its base and large framing moulding to its

Above: This collection box makes an ideal container in which to display fishing memorabilia; the brightly coloured flies and floats look wonderful set among old fishing books, tackle and faded pictures.

Above: While the dado rail is made from moulding, the illusion of a panelled wall was achieved with stencils (page 96), then softly aged for a less graphic effect. The butler's tray was also aged in a lighter tone, then varnished for durability.

top. Then the whole bookcase was given a paint treatment like the walls so that it blended in with the scheme. A modern shop-bought butler's tray and stand were also given an aged look in keeping with the Scottish style. The stand was woodwashed in a soft green, while the tray was painted in a lighter green, then colourwashed in an even paler green for a softer effect.

To create a feeling of warmth and cosiness in the room, a mixture of textures in the form of modern tweeds, plaids and bright mohairs were used; these fabrics also reflect the soft colours of the Highlands. An MDF screen, which was given the same paint treatment as the dado, was covered with a green and cream tartan fabric, and the edges finished with antiqued upholstery studs. The same fabric was also draped over a curtain pole for a soft window treatment. The large easy chair was chosen for its warmth and comfort, while an array of soft blankets added extra cosiness. The small chair was covered with a contemporary tweed and, again, antiqued upholstery studs completed the look.

Scraps of old tweed, plaid and other fabrics were also used to make the appliqué wall-hanging, whose colours and textures echo those used in the room. The transferred images featured in the centre of each fabric patch were handcoloured for an aged look.

This room seemed the ideal place to display woodland finds and hunting trophies as well as all the paraphernalia involved in country pursuits. So, for a finishing touch, a simple box frame was used to make a collection box in which were displayed fishing flies, tackle and other memorabilia as a permanent reminder of days by the river. Among the dark oak furniture, this collection box added a feeling of playfulness.

Below: Old and new furniture work well together in this room. The flatpack bookcase is given an ancestral feel by the addition of mouldings and an ageing paint technique. The fabric-covered screen (page 128) makes an ideal room divider, completely in keeping with the relaxed air of the room.

Above: This small nursing chair was due for re-upholstery (page 126) and a contemporary tweed was chosen to complement the look of the room; antiqued upholstery studs add a suitable finishing touch. The discarded fabric and wadding were used to create a template.

The Mexican look, with its influences of Toltec, Inca, Spanish and French cultures, is at once opulent and simplistic. Religion and superstition are often vividly apparent in many forms of Mexican decoration, but the main focus is family life, and much of the style revolves around the **mexican kitchen**, with the decor being as bold and demonstrative as the families themselves. Typical of Mexican style are vivid colours and patinas found on rough clay walls, cookware and beautifully painted ceramics, resulting in a decor that is both fun to be in and stylishly practical.

mexican kitchen

A new worktop completes the transformation to Mexican style: a pebble-effect formica was chosen as it contained the same hues as the room, and also worked well with the aluminium tiles.

The kitchen needed to be stripped back to basics before the transformation could begin, so all the doors were removed from the units. Then the walls and ceiling were painted white to provide a base for the paint finish. A 7.5cm (3in) border was masked off around the window and a triangle design was masked off on either side of the fireplace. The walls were painted with a special aqua pigment paint that gives the same chalky effect of Mexican interiors. Water is added to the paint and it is then applied in random brushstrokes, giving a slightly broken colour effect. When dry, the masking was removed and the window borders and fireplace triangles painted pink. Pink was also chosen for the fireplace alcove and for the back of the wavy shelf section. The paintwork for the windows and door surrounds was painted a rich blue. To complete the wall decoration, striking wall tiles were made by cutting squares of brushed aluminium and sticking them to MDF

Right: Vibrancy and a mix of colours and textures is the key to Mexican style. Its not always necessary to dispose of old doors and units. Clever use of design and paint have saved these from the scrap heap and given them a new lease of life (page 103).

Brightly coloured walls and paintwork, stylish aluminium decoration and an eclectic mix of accessories have been used to create this wonderful Mexican-style kitchen.

Left: The natural niche of the fireplace makes an interesting display area; the green and pink paintwork (page 94) provides the ideal backdrop for a mix of tin and bright plastics. The simple metal table and plastic chairs are inexpensive but add a stylish touch.

squares. These were stuck to the wall with tile adhesive and grouted in the same way as for ordinary ceramic tiles.

The existing floor was a painted laminate, making it the ideal surface for painting. A border of 10cm (4in) was masked off and two coats of bright blue floor paint were applied in the centre. The masking was then removed and the border painted bright red.

Above: An empty space that once held household appliances is put to good use as extra storage by adding some quirky wavy-edged shelves (page 133). This gives a great display area for kitchen utensils.

The unit doors were also painted bright red and a triangular border cut from thin ply glued to the side of each; this was painted with aqua acrylic eggshell. The drawers were transformed with a panel of aluminium and aluminium knobs and handles were attached to the doors for a decorative finishing touch. A new formica worktop was made for the top of the units, and aluminium angle trim was applied to the edges.

A pair of simple shutters was made from lengths of wood which were first scorched and then colourwashed in dilute bright red paint. Dilute paint applied in the direction of the grain will colour the wood while allowing some of the grain to show through.

Below: When the shutters (page 141) are closed and the candles are lit, the glitter of decorative tin creates a romantic evening atmosphere.

Right: Card and tin were used to make these fun bowls (page 115) that serve a variety of uses. The metal strips on the back of the shutters (page 141), which were also recycled, were fixed to the wood with large round-headed roofing clouts.

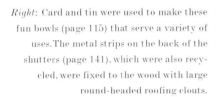

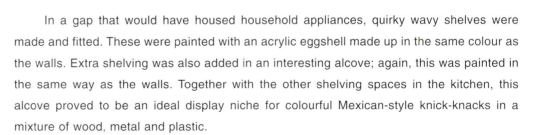

In a gap that would have housed household appliances, quirky wavy shelves were made and fitted. These were painted with an acrylic eggshell made up in the same colour as the walls. Extra shelving was also added in an interesting alcove; again, this was painted in the same way as the walls. Together with the other shelving spaces in the kitchen, this alcove proved to be an ideal display niche for colourful Mexican-style knick-knacks in a mixture of wood, metal and plastic.

In addition to accessorizing with colourful shop-bought accessories, you can have fun with recycling. We made an unusual bowl by weaving together strips of painted corrugated card, and constructed a jolly fruit bowl from an old olive oil can.

Below: This interesting alcove was given an extra dimension by the addition of simple shelves with tiny pillars (page 134). It makes a lovely display area for traditional Mexican paraphernalia, including icons and plastic items. The wall tiles were made from squares of polished aluminium attached to squares of MDF (page 99). Together with the new worktop, these make a chic backdrop to modern metals and frosted glass or plastic.

Above: Choose accessories for the kitchen from a wide variety of wood and metal items to extend the Mexican look further.

Above: A plastic-covered wire basket provides the ideal storage for fun kitchen goods such as this blueberry scouring pad. Look for inexpensive plastics to accessorize Mexican style.

Below: Existing spice shelves are painted in the same colour as the wall and are used for displaying colourful food packaging.

THE MEXICAN KITCHEN **63**

The Scandinavian look is sturdy and practical with an essence of childlike charm. Boxy furniture is a key element, while natural blonde woods or bleached paint effects are common. Fabric also plays an important part in the **swedish bedroom**, with striped and gingham fabric being used in much upholstery and soft furnishings. Traditional crafts and folk art, such as naive wall-paintings in the style of Carl Larsson, Sweden's best loved artist, add highlights of colour in the minimalist interiors.

Left: A charming naivety is added to the room with this Larsson-inspired painted frieze (page 96). The decorative corner cupboard, which echoes the childlike charm, was repainted to match the room scheme.

Above: An old washstand is given a new lease of life with a simple stone paint effect on top and a fresh coat of pale blue emulsion on the base. The metal screen (page 129) is given a new lease of life with bright red gingham.

swedish bedroom

66 THE LOOKS

Above: Fabric plays a major part in the decor of this room. The padded headboard, ticking bolster (page 119) and piles of pillows all add softness to the room and give it a sense of luxury.

Above: Accessorize with a combination of coarse natural linen, rough-textured stone and smooth ceramic to recreate a Scandinavian-style interior.

Above: Plain cupboard doors are easily transformed with fabric insets and mouldings (page 102), while padded throws and cotton bedlinen complement the colour scheme.

Above: This smart ticking bolster (page 119) is given extra crispness and style by the addition of an unusual maltese cross bow in the same fabric at each end.

This light airy bedroom was the ideal space in which to explore the cool and refreshing Scandinavian look. Neat and practical, yet with an air of elegance, this style relies on a mix of textures for its decoration.

To capitalize on the amount of light in the room, I painted the walls and ceiling with pale blue emulsion, a typical colour in the Scandinavian palette. To prevent the blue becoming too cooling, and to give a feeling of movement to an otherwise calm interior, a cheerful red frieze in the style of Larsson was stencilled around the walls.

Several items of furniture, including a washstand, a corner cupboard and an old wooden chair, were also treated with pale soft blue emulsion. The washstand top was then given a stone-effect paint treatment, to introduce another texture into the room.

After establishing the overall colour scheme, more red decoration was required, and this was where fabric, especially gingham and ticking, played a key role. A metal screen was covered with fresh new gingham and the same type of fabric was inserted into plain cupboard doors for added interest. A long bolster was made for the

Above: Linen cafe curtains are hung with brass rings on a brass rod for a smart alternative to nets. They break up the window area, and provide privacy but without losing any light.

Right: Soft furnishings are predominant in this room, creating a real sense of luxury and comfort. The use of fabric is continued with red picture bows (page 108) and the painted gingham lampshade (page 105), which demonstrates how easy it is to create the illusion of fabric with two tones of paint.

Left: The colour scheme for this room is simple yet effective: cool crisp whites, pale blues and soft creams are highlighted with splashes of warm bright reds.

bed, covered with red and white striped ticking and decorated with a smart maltese cross bow; this type of bow has a flatter and crisper design than the usual bow used in soft furnishings.

Linen was used to make simple cafe curtains for the windows. Smart brass rings were stitched on by hand and the curtains were then threaded on to a cafe rail. Linen is an ideal alternative to net, as it allows light to pass through it while at the same time affording privacy to the room. Brocade, a fabric with a more luxurious texture, was used to cover two hat boxes to make an unusual yet simple bedside table. The hat boxes were strung with smart burgundy cord for a decorative finishing touch.

For a novel effect, I painted two plain lampshades with two different shades of red to create the illusion of gingham. Finally, a row of tiny framed prints were hung on red ribbons, each topped with a flat bow, to add to the naive feel of this decorative style.

Right: Clean white furniture looks perfect in a Scandinavian-style room. Here, this chest of drawers is softened by the addition of accessories in a variety of colours and textures. The covered hat boxes make clever and inexpensive bedside tables.

The Indian look incorporates aspects of the richly decorated Hindu temples, the ornate Mughal palaces, the elegant Raj decor, and the rustic style of Kashmiri homes. Yet, although it is both colourful and exciting, Indian style contains at its heart the spirituality of Muslim and Hindu cultures, resulting in powerful yet calm interiors. The **kashmiri bedroom** re-creates the essence of India with its gorgeously coloured silks and paisley furnishings, dark wooden accessories, and brass idols and gods. It is a place in which to light candles and incense, and dream of faraway lands.

Right: Indian artefacts and trinkets are here brought together in a niche-style box frame (page 112). You can scour Indian markets and shops for likely items, or collect ornaments from your travels to exhibit in this lovely display.

kashmiri bedroom

Above: Beautiful saris backed with striped Indian cotton (page 125) are draped back on antique stays (page 142) to provide a sun blind which at night can be let down to provide efficient curtaining.

Spice-coloured saris and dyed muslins have been used to create sumptuous soft furnishings for this Kashmiri bedroom. With the addition of dark wood, gilt and spiritual images, this plain bedroom has become a romantic and relaxing haven exuding the warmth of India.

To set the scene for an Indian makeover, warm colours were required for the ceiling, walls and floor. Red and hot pink were to be used in the soft furnishings, so the ceiling was painted in a soft yellow emulsion, and the walls in a spicy turmeric shade, colours which enhance and blend well with warming reds. The window frame and other paintwork were given a coat of deep pink terracotta satinwood to enhance the walls. The old carpet was removed and a dark coir matting fitted in its place in keeping with the natural spice colours.

With the basics complete, the fun began with the accessories. Richly coloured silk saris bought in a local market were backed with an Indian striped cotton in deep red and gold and used as curtains. A shaped pelmet was cut and painted in deep terracotta, then dry-brushed in a lighter tone. Studs were added for a finishing touch. A simple curtain pole was secured above the window and the pelmet was fitted over the top, attached to brackets. The sari curtains were hung by being wrapped over the curtain pole, then draped around antiqued curtain stays on each side of the window. In this way, both sides

72 THE LOOKS

Right: A plain flatpack bed was adapted and given an Indian-style look by replacing the existing corner posts with carved timber posts (page 138). Dyed muslin sewn in strips makes a romantic draped canopy (page 129).

Right: This small throw for the chest was quickly and easily made from a sari backed with striped cotton. The tassel, made from sprayed hemp twine (page 117), adds a decorative finishing touch.

of the curtain are visible at once – the striped cotton sun blind and the colourful sari curtains.

The bed became the centrepiece of the room. The original posts were replaced with taller ones which, in characteristic Indian style, were taller at the base of the bed than at the head. The new posts were roughly carved, surmounted by round finials, then stained with a combination of woodstain and wood wax for the authentic deep wood colour so often seen in Indian palaces. A striped filmy bed canopy was made from lengths of dyed muslin in hot pink and cinnamon, which were stitched together before being hung over dowels attached to the ceiling. More saris were chosen to make several sumptuous Kashmiri-style cushions for the bed, and colourful matching throws for the bed and the Indian chest at its foot. The abundance of soft furnishings, drapes and hangings creates a relaxing and romantic room.

Left: A shop-bought pouffe and junk-shop chair were re-covered in paisley-stamped suedette (pages 126-7). Old bannister rails were cut down and stained to make authentic Indian-style candle sconces (page 105).

Right: Gorgeously coloured and embroidered Indian fabrics provide a wealth of choice for soft furnishings.

Other items of furniture also received the Indian treatment. A modern pouffe was re-covered in suedette stamped with a paisley design in gold. A junk-shop chair was also given a new lease of life by being re-covered in the same stamped fabric, then its frame was painted black and gilded with bronze gilt cream, in keeping with the rich, dark colouring of the room. To add to the dark wood furnishings, tall candle sconces were made from old bannisters which were then stained with woodstain and wax.

Finally, to pay homage to the spiritual core of India, a decorative niche was made. This was filled with a variety of colourful Indian trinkets and artefacts, found by scouring through market stalls and Indian stores. The finished item adds a sense of peace and tranquillity to the bedroom.

Right: Sumptuous saris and Indian shawls were used to make tasselled cushions (page 117) and a throw for the bed (page 131) for a sense of real luxury.

The French look is crisp, smart and stylish, often with a hint of naughtiness, reflecting the French way of life. Luxury and chic are the keywords of this decorative style, with old and new French furnishings and accessories being combined to achieve a feeling of opulence with a hint of delicacy. In the **parisian boudoir**, pastel colours matched with white and silver are the starting points, while crisp linen and floaty silk soften the decor and add a touch of femininity. Ideal for the bedroom, the French look is romantic and relaxing, while still remaining stylish and functional.

A plush velvet-covered chaise gives a suitably glamorous touch to the room. Sumptuous cushions add further luxury, making it the ideal place to recline and pamper yourself.

Right: Painted lilac stripes and dainty strings of hanging beads give this once plain lampshade (page 104) a sophisticated charm.

The dimensions of this room with its large bay window made it a delight to transform into a Parisian boudoir. Billowy drapes, spotty voiles and a mix of silver, glass and warm walnut blend to create a look that is both glamorous and coolly sophisticated.

parisian boudoir

Above: This mirror with its ornate moulding is perfect in a boudoir. It was gilded with aluminium leaf and softly aged (page 111). Long glass vases with single stems are a simple yet stunning way to style the room.

To set the scene, the walls were painted with two coats of luxury lavender matt emulsion, while the picture rail, window frames and skirting were left white. The ceiling was painted in a soft grey, which was complemented by a dove grey, short-pile carpet. This initial decoration produced a clean crisp backdrop to the room, which was now yearning to be softened by fabrics and delicate accessories.

To soften the windows, thick voile was decorated with a cork-stamped design and hung on net curtain wires, and opulent drapes were made and lined to give a dramatic backdrop to the room. A decorative chaise frame upholstered in a deep violet velvet made an extravagant reclining spot; this was further enhanced by the addition of several plump cushions in toning fabrics.

A wardrobe and dressing table found in a junk shop were given a touch of glamour with a distressed paint technique, giving them a crisp yet softly aged look in lilac and grey. New handles and knobs completed the effect. An unpainted MDF correspondence table was also treated to the same paint effect.

Some existing storage in the form of wooden drawers from a draper's shop introduced walnut into the scheme. These were given a cunning facelift by the insertion of colour copies of the curtain fabric and cut pieces of wrapping paper. A tailor's dummy with a perfect walnut base, which matched the wood of the drawers, was used to display period clothing.

Left: This wardrobe was an inexpensive junk-shop find transformed with an aged paint technique (page 136) and new handles. Its gently curved top made an ideal display place for old luggage and hat boxes. Chic period clothing, nonchalantly displayed on padded hangers, adds to the boudoir look.

Left: This small correspondence table was given a soft aged effect using shades of grey and lilac. The small lamp base is transformed by the use of blown glass balls (page 104). The lampshade was decorated using filler applied with a piping bag (page 104).

With the furniture in place, accessories were required to complete the look. Chrome, silver leaf and soft silks were the key elements. A plain pole standard and side light were given a sophisticated touch by threading glass baubles on to their bases, while the plain white shades were decorated with stripes, beads and piping. Other wooden and glass wall lights were gilded with silver leafing. Continuing the use of silver, a large gold mirror was gilded with aluminium leaf to give the illusion of silver, before being softly aged with a lilac glaze, while small metal cafe tables were given a stylish chrome-effect finish. Other accessories included walnut and chrome frames, which were used to display old period prints, and delicate glassware, both old and new.

Right: An otherwise ordinary dressing table was adapted by the addition of new legs, a shaped top and elegant knobs (page 136). A soft aged effect using wax resist techniques was used to decorate it and bring it into line with the room. An array of baubles, perfumery and pretty potted plants are displayed to continue the predominantly feminine feel.

82 THE LOOKS

Left: A draper's unit is the ideal place to store lingerie and other clothing; the warm wood works well with the cool lilac. Look for antique clothing, hat boxes and luggage that not only add glamour but extra storage too. A tailor's dummy is used to display clothing, while pieces of the curtain fabric are used to hide some drawer fronts where the contents are not so decorative.

The Greek look comprises understated elegance and classical lines. While the ruins of Ancient Greece still exert an architectural inspiration, contemporary homes are simpler in design and are influenced more by the sun and sea. The intense blue skies are reflected in the colours used in the **aegean washroom**, while white-painted walls reflect the sun on the outside and keep the rooms cool and fresh on the inside. Cool tiles, earthy stonework and glass predominate in this minimalist yet relaxed style, with ornate icons and mosaic often the only visible ornament.

Below: These simple punched tin lanterns (page 106) were decorated with the St John cross motif. They were then secured with pop rivets and patinated before being placed over a nightlight for those romantic candlelit baths.

A compact bathroom proved to be an ideal target for the Greek look. With its cool white interior, textured walls and refreshing blue decoration, it soon developed the feel of a light and airy washroom, reflecting the colours of the Greek landscape.

aegean washroom

White and blue were to be the starting points in the bathroom; luckily, the bathroom suite was white, which removed the necessity for a costly conversion. The rest of the room, however, had to be completely stripped before the decorating could begin.

Aqua emulsion was chosen for the ceiling and window inset to set the scene. Then, to complement the colour, a screen was built using cool blue glass bricks; this divided the bath from the sink and, with the addition of shelves on one side, solved the bathroom storage problem without taking up too much space. A line was marked 40cm (16in) above the bath and sink and this area was decorated with mosaic in shades of aqua blue; the deep windowsill was also treated to the same mosaic effect.

Textured white emulsion was brushed randomly over the remaining wall areas to create the effect of rough plaster so often seen in Aegean interiors. To break up the starkness of this

Above: The glass brick screen (page 145) makes an ideal partition between bath and sink. The aged pewter mirror frame (page 111) sits well against the white walls.

A jewelled St John cross (page 110) adorns the wall, echoing the smaller stencilled motifs bordering the walls and floor (page 95). The glass brick screen (page 145) provides a framework for handy storage; this screen was also given a textured paint effect (page 94).

Above: The old sink unit doors were removed and a glass brick inserted in each (page 140). The sink top and the splashback were all transformed with mosaic in varying shades of blue (page 98). A mirror frame covered with pewter (page 111) added to the scheme.

Below: Cool zinc was used for an inset in the bath surround (page 102) while the outside frame was painted in a deep blue emulsion before being sealed. The zinc was sanded and rubbed with wire wool to soften the high tech effect. The stencilled cross border (page 95) was stencilled on the floor using aqua floor paint.

Above: The deep windowsill was decorated with blue mosaic tiles while the blind for the window (page 126) was made from a dyed pink lace tablecloth and a roller blind kit to echo the colour of flowering bougainvillaea.

effect, a border of St John crosses was stencilled around the top of the walls in the same aqua blue as used on the ceiling. The St John cross is a motif that recurs in much Grecian decoration; originally, it was the cross of the Chevaliers, or Knights Templars, who lived in the old town of Rhodes during the Middle Ages. The same motif was stencilled on the floor with matching aqua floor paint to create a border around the room.

Once the walls and floor were finished, it was time to revamp the furniture. The old sink doors and bath surround were removed. Glass bricks were inserted into the sink doors and the doors then painted with ultramarine blue emulsion. A zinc panel was attached to the bath surround, secured with a neat moulding and the surround painted in deep blue emulsion. Lanterns made from punched tin echoed the metallic feel.

A wall-hanging icon in the shape of a St John cross was made from MDF and decorated with glass nuggets, linking the stencilled crosses on walls and floor, and adding to the blue decoration. To emulate the beautiful colours of bougainvillaea so often seen in Greece, a lace tablecloth was dyed bright pink and made up into a neat roller blind for the window. To complete the look, the room was accessorized with contemporary chrome and steel pieces, dyed straw, and natural sponges and soaps.

the

part two

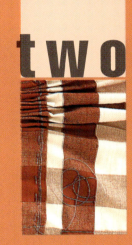

projects

page 24 page 16

decorative projects

This lacquered red screen featuring writhing découpaged dragons (page 19) adds an authentic touch to the Chinese living room.

aged plaster wall finish (page 26)

You will need:
- Emulsion paint: white, terracotta
- A 10cm (4in) household paintbrush
- A large container
- Acrylic scumble glaze
- Boards primed with white emulsion paint
- A large softening brush

Apply two coats of white emulsion paint to the surface, allowing two to three hours' drying time between each coat. In a large container, mix 6 parts acrylic scumble glaze with 1 part terracotta emulsion; 1 litre (1¾ pints) of mixed glaze covers 15m (16½yd) square. Stir well.

Before applying the paint effect on the surface, practise on primed boards to gain confidence.

Dip the tip of a large brush in the glaze and apply it to the surface with random brushstrokes. Working quickly, use a softening brush to skim over the glazed surface with the tips of the bristles to soften out any brushstrokes. Work in 1m (1⅛yd) round sections and avoid any squared-off edges. Keep the edges wet and try to complete a whole wall before stopping for a break. If working with someone else, make sure you follow each other and that the technique remains the same. Allow to dry for two to three hours.

parchment-effect wall finish (page 20)

You will need:
- Emulsion paint: parchment, white
- A 10cm (4in) household paintbrush
- Acrylic scumble glaze
- A container
- A large lily bristle softening brush
- A cloth
- Antique pine tinted wood wax

Apply two coats of parchment emulsion to the surface, allowing each coat to dry for two to three hours. Combine 6 parts acrylic scumble glaze with 1 part white emulsion paint in a container and mix well. Dip the tip of a paintbrush into the glaze and brush it over the surface in random strokes; this provides a broken colour effect which allows some of the base coat to show through.

Working quickly, go over the wet glaze with a softening brush, lightly skimming it over the surface to soften the brushstrokes.

Allow to dry for two to three hours. Using a cloth, rub a thin coat of antique pine tinted wax over the surface to seal and antique it. You might find it helpful to practise this technique first on a board before applying the glaze on the wall.

page 84 page 56 page 56 page 84

textured wall finish (page 86)

You will need:
A large container
White emulsion paint
Fine-textured powder filler
An offcut of batten
A 10cm (4in) household paintbrush

In a large container, mix together 2 parts white emulsion and 1 part fine-textured powder filler. The best way to do this to avoid lumps is to add the powder filler gradually to the paint, stirring with a piece of batten until the filler is thoroughly combined.

Using a large paintbrush, apply the mixture to the wall in random brushstrokes. Allow to dry for three hours. Then paint a coat of neat white emulsion over the top, working it well into the textured surface, and allow to dry for a further two to three hours.

mexican wall finish (page 58)

You will need:
White emulsion paint
A 10cm (4in) household paintbrush
A craft knife
A cutting mat
Ticket or very thin card
Adhesive stencil spray
A container
Chalky-finish paint: aqua, pink
Low-tack masking tape
A small artist's brush

Paint the surface with a coat of white emulsion and leave to dry.

Using a craft knife and working on a cutting mat, cut some triangles out of ticket card and attach them in a vertical row down the wall, securing with adhesive stencil spray.

In a container, mix 6 parts aqua paint with 2 parts water. Stir well. Dip the tip of a wide brush into the mixture and apply it over the surface, brushing in all directions; this produces a broken colour effect, allowing some of the base colour to show through the aqua paint.

Carefully remove the triangular stencils and allow the first colour to dry. Then stick masking tape around each triangle up to the outside edge and fill in the triangles with pink paint using a small artist's brush. Carefully remove the masking tape and allow the paint to dry.

woodwashed surface (page 61)

You will need:
Emulsion paint
A container
A 7.5cm (3in) household paintbrush
4 door hinges and screw attachments

Pour some emulsion paint into a container, and add water to it a little at a time. The mix is approximately 2 parts water to 6 parts paint. Test the woodwash out on a piece of spare wood before applying it on a wooden surface. The grain of the wood should still be visible through the coloured wash. Brush the wash over the wood, always in the direction of the grain. Allow to dry, then apply a second coat of woodwash for a more pronounced colour. Allow to dry for ten to fifteen minutes. As the woodwash is fairly thin, it will sink into the surface of the wood quite quickly.

stencilled surface (page 89)

You will need:
Coarse-grade sandpaper
Emulsion paint: white, aqua
A 7.5cm (3in) household paintbrush
A cutting mat
Stencil film
Masking tape
A permanent pen
A craft knife
A pencil
A tape measure (optional)
Stencil spray (optional)
A 1cm (½in) round fitch brush
Paper towels

Smooth down the surface with sandpaper. Paint two coats of white emulsion over the top, allowing the first coat to dry for two to three hours before applying the second.

Making a stencil

Photocopy the template on page 151 and, if necessary, enlarge it to the desired size. Lay the photocopy on a cutting mat and place the stencil film over the top, securing on each side with masking tape. Draw over the outline of the motif with a permanent pen. Then, using a craft knife, carefully cut around the outline of the St John cross to make the stencil; discard the cut-out piece.

Stencilling

Decide where you want to position each stencil, and mark each place with a pencil dot; you can do this by eye or by using a tape measure. Lay the stencil over each mark in turn, securing with masking tape or stencil spray. Dip a fitch brush in aqua emulsion, dab off excess paint on a paper towel, then stipple the paint through the stencil. Repeat for each stencil, dipping the brush in the paint as often as necessary. Do not overload the brush with paint, as paint may bleed beneath the stencil, spoiling the effect. Carefully remove the stencil and allow to dry for one to two hours.

DECORATIVE PROJECTS

page 52   page 64   page 30

trompe-l'oeil panelling (page 53)

You will need:
- *A 5cm (2in) household paintbrush*
- *Emulsion paint: deep green, light green, dark green*
- *Stencil card*
- *A fine permanent pen*
- *A straight edge*
- *A cutting mat*
- *A craft knife*
- *A pencil (optional)*
- *Low-tack masking tape*
- *A spirit level*
- *Two 1.5cm (½in) round fitch brushes or stencil brushes*
- *Paper towels*

This faux paint effect is especially effective below a chair rail to suggest panelling. First, paint the base coat of deep green emulsion and leave to dry.

Making the stencils

Enlarge the template on page 151 and transfer the two L-shapes on to stencil card using a fine permanent pen and a straight edge. Mitre each corner on both L-shapes so that when the two stencils are placed together, with one L-shape upturned, they make a rectangle. Place the stencil card on a cutting mat and cut out both L-shapes with a craft knife.

Stencilling

Work out the placing of the panelling below the dado rail either by eye or by measuring and marking the wall with a pencil. Place the first L-shape on the wall and secure with low-tack masking tape. Use a spirit level to check that it is level. Dip the tip of the fitch brush into light green emulsion and dab off any excess on a paper towel. Then stipple through the stencil, working away from the edges. Remove the stencil; allow the paint to dry for an hour.

Next, position the second up-turned L on the wall so that it butts up to the first L-shape, and stipple dark green emulsion through the stencil. Remove the stencil and allow to dry. Repeat along the wall.

Colourwashing

Add a touch of dark green emulsion and burnt umber acrylic to acrylic satin varnish. Paint this over the walls in vertical strokes to age them lightly.

stencilled frieze (page 67)

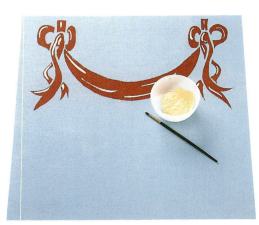

You will need:
- *A sheet of glass*
- *Stencil film*
- *A heated stencil cutter*
- *A pencil*
- *Stencil spray*
- *A stencil brush*
- *Emulsion paint: deep red, cream*
- *Paper towels*
- *An artist's brush*

Photocopy the swag design (see template on page 151) and lay the glass on top of it. Place the sheet of stencil film on top of the glass and make a stencil of the design using a heated stencil cutter (page 97).

Decide where you want the swags to begin on the wall, and mark the position. Lightly spray over the reverse of the stencil with stencil spray. Leave for a few seconds and then attach the stencil to the wall; the spray will hold the stencil in place without removing any paint.

Dip a stencil brush into a pot of deep red paint and dab it on a paper towel to remove excess paint. Holding the stencil brush horizontally, stipple the paint through the stencil, working away from the edges to prevent paint bleeding under the stencil film, until the whole design is covered. Remove the stencil carefully and allow the paint to dry. Then, using an artist's brush and cream paint, carefully paint in extra details on the bow and swag. Leave to dry.

To stencil along the wall to create a frieze, line up the stencil by eye with the first painted bow and swag and repeat the stencilling process.

96 THE PROJECTS

stencilled mosaic-effect wall (page 32)

You will need:
A piece of glass
Stencil film
A heated stencil cutter
Emulsion paint: cream, green, orange
5cm (2in) household paintbrushes
Stencil spray
Stencil brushes
Paper towels
A pencil
Antique pine brushing wax

Enlarge the Moroccan star and interlocking cross template (page 150) on a photocopier so that each motif is about 6cm (2½in) high.

Making a stencil

Make a stencil of four of the main star motifs, by first laying a piece of glass on the photocopy. Cover this with a sheet of stencil film. Warm up a heated stencil cutter for five minutes, then use it to draw over the outlines of the stars; press out the cut pieces. Repeat to make a stencil of the interlocking cross panel. Finally, cut out a single-image stencil for each part of the pattern, to use in small spaces.

Prepare the area of wall to be stencilled by first painting it with two coats of cream emulsion, allowing the first coat to dry for two hours before applying the second coat. Allow the second coat to dry.

Stencilling

Spray the back of the first stencil panel with stencil spray, leave it for a few seconds, then attach it to the wall where you want to begin stencilling; the stencil spray will attach the stencil securely to the wall without harming the paint beneath. Dip a stencil brush into green emulsion paint, wipe off any excess on a paper towel, then stipple through the stencil, working away from the cut edge to prevent bleed. When you have finished, carefully remove the stencil and reposition it further along the wall, ensuring that there is enough space in between the first and second stencils to insert the interlocking stencil. Either align the stencil by eye or make pencilled registration marks on the wall to follow. Repeat the stencilling all along the wall and allow the stars to dry for one hour.

Then insert the interlocking panels and repeat the stencilling, this time using orange emulsion, until the wall is covered with orange crosses. If there are any awkward areas that remain uncovered, use the single-image stencils to stencil them. Allow the second set of stencilling to dry for an hour. Then dry-brush the wax over the surface to age the wall. This will set after 15 minutes to produce a hard-wearing finish.

page 24   page 84   page 56   page 24

trompe-l'oeil arch (page 26)

You will need:

A pencil
A straight edge
Masking tape
Emulsion paint: grey, pale yellow, pale brown, white
A 5cm (2in) household paintbrush
Aged plaster glaze (page 93)
A 7.5cm (3in) household paintbrush
A large softening brush
A compass with extender arm
Medium-grade sandpaper
Tracing paper
A Pompeiian source book
Assorted artist's brushes

Working below the picture rail, and using a pencil and straight edge, mark the outer edges of the arch, which is 140cm (56in) wide, with a vertical line from the picture rail to the skirting. Measure 25cm (10in) in from each side and draw another vertical line at each side. Mask up to these lines on both sides of the arch. Dry-brush each side with grey emulsion.

When dry, remove the masking tape, then mask up to the centre of the arch. Apply the aged plaster mix to the centre panel (page 93); when dry, remove the tape.

Mark the centre point of the arch at the picture rail. Using a compass with an extender arm, draw a semi-circular shape from the centre, extending to the outside edges of the arch. Then draw two triangular shapes at each top corner above the semi-circle (see template on page 150).

Mask off up to the inside lines of the triangular shapes and dry-brush them with grey emulsion. Allow to dry and remove the tape. Paint the semi-circle with pale yellow emulsion. Lightly sand the surface to soften the paintwork. Mask off the fanlight areas and fill in the pale brown paint in the elliptical shapes with grey emulsion; sand again.

Draw a vertical border design on the wall. Using an artist's brush, fill in the main body with the pale yellow. Fill in the highlights with white paint and the shadows with pale brown.

mosaic splashback (page 86)

You will need:

Mixed blue vitreous tesserae, each tile measuring 20 x 20mm (¾ x ¾in)
A tape measure
A stanley knife
Dark ultramarine tesserae, as above
A cloth
Sugar soap
A flexible spreader
Tile adhesive
A spirit level (optional)
Matchsticks
A sponge
Tile grout

Vitreous tesserae are available in sheets of mixed colours, measuring 30cm (12in) square. To avoid cutting any tiles, ensure that the area of your mosaic matches one or more of the 30cm (12in) square sheets.

Lay out the sheets of tiles, paper-side down. Using a stanley knife, remove a few tiles from each sheet; replace with ultramarine tiles so that the grooved side of the tiles is facing upwards. Using a cloth and sugar soap, clean the area where the mosaic is to be applied; allow to dry.

Applying the tiles

Using a spreader, spread tile adhesive evenly on to the wall over an area as large as a square sheet of tiles. Place a sheet of tiles on to the adhesive, tile-side down, pushing to make sure they stick. Continue to apply tile adhesive and fix the tile sheets on top until the whole area is covered.

Grouting

Allow the mosaic to dry overnight, then soak the backing paper off with a damp sponge. Using a flexible spreader, spread tile grout over the mosaic, pressing it into all the spaces. Wipe off any excess grout with a damp sponge.

aluminium tiles (page 58)

You will need:
Metal ruler
A permanent pen
1 sheet of 2.4 x 1.2m (8 x 4ft) brushed aluminium
1 sheet of 2.4 x 1.2m (8 x 4ft) MDF, 6mm (¼in) thick
An electric chop saw (can be hired from a tool hire store)
Epoxy resin glue
G-clamps
Tile adhesive
Tile spacers
Grey-coloured grout
A flexible spreader
A sponge

These materials are enough to make approximately 100 tiles, each one measuring 10.5cm (4⅛in) square.

Measure and mark out 10.5cm (4⅛in) squares on the reverse of a sheet of aluminium using a permanent pen. Repeat on the MDF. Cut out all the squares using a chop saw, which enables you to chop several pieces of wood simultaneously. Secure the aluminium squares to the MDF squares with epoxy resin glue; hold in place for two hours with g-clamps for the glue to bond.

Apply tile adhesive over a small area of the wall and press the tiles into the adhesive, MDF-side down, using tile spacers in between each tile for correct spacing. Continue applying adhesive and fixing tiles in position until the wall is covered. Allow to dry overnight.

Mix up the grout following the manufacturer's instructions. Using a spreader, apply the grout over the tiles, pushing it into the spaces between the tiles. Remove excess grout with a dampened sponge. Allow to dry for six hours, then remove any further residue with a damp sponge.

painted canvas floorcloth (page 28)

You will need:
4 x 3.3m (4¼ x 3½yd) duck canvas, 250g (9oz)
Scissors
Pins
A sewing machine with a denim needle
Matching strong thread
A tape measure
Aged plaster glaze (page 93)
A 10cm (4in) household paintbrush
A large softening brush
Emulsion paint: dark peach, grey, pale yellow, ochre, terracotta
A 2.5cm (1in) flat artist's brush
A pencil and a compass
Transfer paper
Water-based matt acrylic varnish
A varnish brush

Make up a canvas panel as for the blind in the beach house (page 125). The size of this floorcloth is 180 x 140cm (72 x 56in).

Apply the glaze over the cloth following the instructions on page 93 and allow to dry. Approximately 10cm (4in) from the edge, paint a line of alternate peach and grey squares measuring 2.5cm (1in) using a flat brush; continue all around the edge of the canvas.

Using a pencil and compass, draw a circle in the centre of the canvas measuring 45cm (18in) in diameter. Enlarge the template (page 152) and transfer it to the centre of the circle. Paint the design in coloured squares using the photograph as reference, then fill in the circle with pale yellow and ochre squares. Paint a ring of grey and peach squares all around the circle, and outside this ring, paint another ring of terracotta squares. Allow the paint to dry.

To complete the canvas floorcloth, apply two coats of matt acrylic varnish over the entire cloth, allowing the first coat to dry before applying the second. This will give the finished floorcloth a tough, durable finish.

page 44   page 44

Framed silhouettes (page 49) copied from an 18th century sourcebook make ideal styling details in the Georgian parlour, but it is fun to make your own of friends and relatives.

100 THE PROJECTS

inked silhouettes (page 49)

You will need:
- *A Polaroid camera and film*
- *Tracing paper*
- *Thick cartridge or watercolour paper*
- *A pencil*
- *Black ink*
- *A fine artist's brush*
- *A frame*

First stand the person you wish to make a silhouette of against a white or light-coloured background so that they are exactly in profile. Photograph with a Polaroid camera until you have a clear image. When the picture is dry, take a piece of tracing paper and lay it over the image. Using a pencil, carefully trace the person's profile, including as much detail as you can. Decide if you want to enlarge the image on a photocopier or keep it as it is. If you do want to make a larger silhouette, you will have to trace over the photocopy of the image on another piece of tracing paper.

Turn the tracing paper over and retrace your lines on the reverse side. Turn the image back to its original side and position the paper on cartridge or watercolour paper. Go over the lines once more with the pencil to transfer the image.

Fill in the image with black ink using a thin artist's brush. You can add more detail by enhancing features like eyelashes and hair. When dry, place the silhouette in a frame of your choice.

hand-tinted and aged prints (page 49)

You will need:
- *A sourcebook of Georgian engravings*
- *A craft knife*
- *Felt pens in a selection of colours*
- *Antique pine and medium mahogany water-based woodstain*
- *An old container*
- *A natural sea sponge*

Choose your image from a copyright-free sourcebook and enlarge it to the required size using a photocopier. With a craft knife, trim the photocopied image to the exact size you require. Now take some felt pens in a selection of colours and colour in elements of the main images. In this case, I picked out the ladies' dresses and the gentleman's frockcoats. This works better than colouring in the whole print.

Pour 1 tbsp of antique pine water-based woodstain and 1 tbsp of medium mahogany woodstain into a container and mix well. If your print is very large you will need to increase the amount of woodstain you use, keeping the same proportions. Dampen a natural sea sponge with some water and wring out well. Dip the sponge into the stain and lightly wipe it over the surface of the print, spreading the woodstain out well. Allow to dry for 20–30 minutes before framing. Either frame the print or use it as a motif for découpage.

page 64   page 84   page 56   page 16

fabric insets on cupboard doors (page 67)

You will need:

Rubber gloves
A cloth
Sugar soap
A pencil
A straight edge
A 5cm (2in) household paintbrush
White acrylic wood primer
Cream acrylic satinwood paint
A tape measure
A small saw
Two 2m (2¼yd) lengths of moulding
A protracter
A mitre block
Scissors
4m (4½yd) gingham fabric
Adhesive craft spray
Wood glue
Panel pins
A hammer
A small artist's brush

These materials are sufficient to make two fabric insets for double full-length doors, each door measuring 195cm (78in) high and 80cm (32in) wide.

Wearing rubber gloves, clean the doors with sugar soap and a cloth to remove any dirt and grease. Leave to dry thoroughly.

Using a pencil and straight edge, mark a line 12cm (5in) in from the edge around all four sides of each door. Paint a coat of acrylic wood primer over the sides of each door, up to the pencilled line and allow to dry for one to two hours. Then apply a coat of cream acrylic satinwood paint over the same area and again leave to dry.

Measure the pencilled lines on the doors and saw a length of moulding to fit each line exactly. Using a protractor and pencil, mark 45° angles at each end of the moulding lengths to aid mitring. Using a mitre block and saw, mitre the ends of the moulding using the marked angles as guides, so that the pieces of moulding will fit together in a frame shape. Check that the angles are correct. Prime the moulding lengths with acrylic wood primer and, when dry, apply a coat of cream satinwood paint on top.

Measure the size of the pencilled rectangle on the doors and cut out fabric to size for both doors. Spray both the door and the reverse of the fabric with craft spray, then carefully lay the fabric in the marked inset, making sure it is taut and flat. Place the lengths of moulding over the marked lines, covering the edges of the fabric, and attach in place using wood glue. Tap in panel pins at intervals around the moulding for extra security. Using a small artist's brush, lightly paint over the ends of the panel pins with cream acrylic satinwood to disguise them.

zinc bath panel (page 89)

You will need:

A wooden bath surround
A screwdriver
A permanent pen
A straight edge
A sheet of tin-plated zinc
Tin snips and epoxy resin glue
A mitre block and saw
Lengths of semi-circle batten
Wood glue and masking tape
Panel pins and a hammer
White acrylic wood primer
Emulsion paint: ultramarine
2.5cm (1in) paintbrushes
Satin acrylic varnish
Wire wool
A cloth and clear furnishing wax

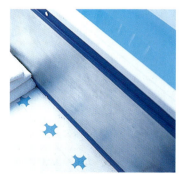

Remove the bath surround with a screwdriver. Using a permanent pen and a straight edge, mark a line around the bath surround, 10cm (4in) from the edge, to form a rectangle. Mark out a rectangle the same size on tin-plated zinc; cut it out with tin snips.

Coat the inner rectangle on the surround and one side of the zinc rectangle with epoxy resin glue, then stick the zinc on to the surround. Cut a length of semi-circle batten into four pieces with mitred corners to provide a frame for the zinc; it should overlap the zinc by 6mm (¼in). Secure the frame in place around the zinc using wood glue and panel pins.

Mask off the edges of the zinc, and paint the surround and frame with acrylic wood primer. When dry, apply two coats of ultramarine emulsion, then two coats of satin acrylic varnish and allow to dry. Remove the masking tape.

Gently rub wire wool over the zinc which will age it. Seal the zinc by rubbing on clear wax; leave to dry then buff up with a cloth. Re-attach the bath surround.

102 THE PROJECTS

decorated kitchen cupboard doors (page 61)

You will need:

Tracing paper
A pencil
1m (1¼yd) square sheet of MDF, 6mm (¼in) thick
A jigsaw
Medium-grade sandpaper
Epoxy resin glue
G-clamps
White oil-based wood primer
Two 5cm (2in) household paintbrushes
Eggshell paint: red, green
A 10cm (4in) paint tray and sponge roller
Satin polyurethane varnish
A varnish brush
1m (1¼yd) square sheet of polished aluminium
Metal ruler
A drill
Aluminium knobs and screws
A screwdriver

The materials listed above are sufficient to decorate eight kitchen cupboard doors measuring 70cm (28in) high and 47cm (19in) wide, each with drawers measuring 47cm (19in) wide and 20cm (8in) high.

Using the template on page 151, transfer the zigzag shape twice on to MDF. Cut them out using a jigsaw, and rub down any rough edges with sandpaper. Secure the shapes to the outside edges of the door with epoxy resin glue and secure in place with g-clamps. Allow to dry for two hours. Paint the drawer front and door with a coat of white oil-based primer and allow to dry for four hours. Then apply two coats of red paint, allowing each coat to dry for four hours. Pour the green paint into a paint tray and roller the raised zigzag shapes with two coats of the green paint. When dry, apply two coats of varnish over the door, allowing four to five hours between each coat.

Using a jigsaw, cut a piece of aluminium measuring 44 x 14cm (17½ x 5½in). Secure this to the drawer front with epoxy resin glue; clamp for two hours. Mark a centre point on the drawer, drill a pilot hole, then attach a knob. Repeat for the remaining doors.

découpaged screen (page 21)

You will need:

Tracing paper
Two 2.4 x 1.2m (8 x 4ft) sheets of MDF, 10mm (⅜in) thick
A pencil
A straight edge
A tape measure
A protective face mask
A workmate
A jigsaw
Medium-grade sandpaper
Pink water-based wood primer
A 5cm (2in) household paintbrush
Red water-based gloss paint
Black and white photocopies
A cutting mat
A scalpel or small craft knife
Yellow water-based ink
A large flat artist's brush
A 2.5cm (1in) round fitch brush
PVA glue
Antique pine tinted wood varnish
Clear varnish (optional)
4 hinges, 5cm (2in) long, and screw fittings
A drill
A screwdriver

The screen measures 1.5m (5ft) high and 1.35m (4ft 6in) wide. Each panel is 40cm (16in) wide, with the outside panels being 7cm (3in) wider each side at the top.

Enlarge the template of the pediment (page 155) and transfer the image on to MDF. Extend the base of the pediment to the required depth of the screen, and divide into three panels. Wearing a face mask, and securing the MDF in a workmate, cut out the panels with a jigsaw; sand rough edges.

Lacquering

Paint each panel with a coat of pink primer and allow to dry for two hours. Apply up to three coats of red gloss paint, allowing each coat to dry for two to three hours; this will produce a glossy finish.

Découpage

Cut out the black and white photocopies with a scalpel. Mix some yellow water-based ink with a little water; paint this over the image and allow to dry. Apply PVA glue on to the reverse of each image, and stick the circular dragon to the centre panel and the rearing dragons on each side panel. Smooth out any wrinkles.

When dry, dilute PVA in the proportion of 1 part water to 3 parts PVA and apply this over the surface to seal. Allow to dry for one hour. Apply tinted wood varnish over the top, working in vertical strokes. When dry, attach the four hinges to the sides of the central panel. Then attach the two side panels to the hinges.

page 78 | page 78 | page 64 | page 70

glass ball lamp base (page 82)

You will need:
A long-stemmed lamp base
Masking tape
Newspaper
Chrome spray paint
A small screwdriver
Blown and drilled clear glass balls (available from fishing suppliers)

Mask off the electrical section of the lamp base and part of the flex with masking tape. Cover the work surface with newspaper for protection, then spray two or three even coats of chrome car spray paint over the lamp base, holding the can 30cm (12in) away from the surface; spray in sweeping movements to avoid clogging or paint drips forming. Allow to dry, then remove the masking tape.

Using a small screwdriver, detach the electrical fitting from the top of the lamp base. Then slide four or five clear glass balls on to the stem and secure the electrical piece back into place to complete.

piped and striped lampshades (page 82)

You will need:
A container
Powder filler
A piping bag and nozzle or a greaseproof paper cone
2 standard fabric lampshades
Emulsion paint: white, lilac
A 2.5cm (1in) household paintbrush
A pencil
A tape measure (optional)
Masking tape
A needle
Nylon thread
28 lilac beads
28 lilac sequins
56 clear beads
A lighter
Scissors

Piped lampshade
In a container mix together powder filler with water until it is the consistency of cake icing. Pour some of this mixture into a piping bag with a nozzle, or a cone made from greaseproof paper with the end snipped off. Ensure that the lampshade is securely placed and pipe wavy random lines of filler over the surface. Allow to dry for two to three hours, then apply up to three coats of white emulsion paint over the lampshade, allowing each coat to dry for two hours before applying the next.

Striped and beaded lampshade
The materials listed above will make 28 drops of beads around a lampshade. Paint two coats of white emulsion over the surface of the lampshade, allowing two hours' drying time between each coat. Divide the shade into eight sections vertically, and mark with a pencil; this can be done by eye or with the help of a tape measure. Mask off alternate lines. Apply lilac paint on alternate sections. Remove the masking tape and allow to dry.

Using a needle, prick through 28 holes approximately 2.5cm (1in) apart all the way around the base of the shade. Take a 7cm (3in) length of nylon thread and make a knot at one end of it. Thread on a lilac bead, a sequin and then two clear beads. Pass the end of the thread through a hole in the lampshade, then take it back through the beads and out at the knotted end. Using a lighter, burn the knot to melt the nylon and secure it, then snip off any excess with scissors. Repeat to thread 27 further drops of beads.

gingham lampshade (page 68)

You will need:

A paper lampshade
Emulsion paint: cream, red, deep red
2.5cm (1in) household paintbrushes
A tape measure
A pencil
Masking tape, 2.5cm (1in) wide

Paint the lampshade cream and allow to dry for one to two hours. Measure the circumference of the top of the shade and divide it into equal segments, approximately 3.5cm (1½in) wide, marking the top of each segment with a pencil. To create the vertical stripes, stick masking tape between two marked points vertically down to the bottom of the lampshade. Mask off every alternate segment in this way all the way round the lampshade.

Then, using a household paintbrush, apply red emulsion over the unmasked areas, taking care to work away from the edges to prevent the paint bleeding beneath the tape. Allow to dry for one to two hours, then carefully remove the masking tape.

Lay the lampshade on its side and mask off the horizontal stripes in the same way as before, ensuring that the top of the lampshade is unmasked. Apply deep red emulsion to the unmasked areas. Allow to dry for one to two hours before removing the masking tape.

free-standing candle sconce (page 76)

You will need:

A tape measure
A pencil
A large bannister pole
A saw
A compass
A piece of softwood, 2.5cm (1in) thick
A workmate
A jigsaw
A drill
Screws, 4cm (1½in) long
A screwdriver
Woodfiller
Medium-grade sandpaper
Cloths
Indian rosewood woodstain
Mahogany wood wax
A nail
A match or lighter
A chunky candle

Measure and mark with a line on the bannister the length you wish the sconce to be. Saw off the excess bannister. Using a compass and pencil, draw out two circles on softwood, one 10cm (4in) in diameter and one 18cm (7in) in diameter. Secure the softwood in a workmate and, using a jigsaw, cut out the circles. Drill a pilot hole into the centre of the smaller circle and insert a screw. With the central screw pointing upwards, secure the smaller circle to the top of the bannister with two screws, having first drilled a pilot hole for each screw. The central upturned screw will be used to secure the candle.

You may find that there is a large rectangular hole at the base of the bannister for attachment to the stairs; fill this with woodfiller, allow it to dry and then rub it down with sandpaper. Secure the larger softwood circle to the base of the sconce with two screws.

Using a cloth, apply a coat of Indian rosewood woodstain over the entire candle sconce in the direction of the grain, and allow to dry. Then apply a layer of mahogany wood wax over the sconce, in the direction of the grain. Leave this for 15 minutes, then buff it up with a cloth.

Before placing a candle on the sconce, first heat a nail in the flame from a match or lighter and then push it up through the centre of the candle base; this will provide a hole for the screw and will ensure that the candle does not crack.

DECORATIVE PROJECTS **105**

| page 84 | page 24 | page 16 | page 24 |

punched tin lantern (page 89)

You will need:
A4 tracing paper
A pencil
A permanent pen
A4 sheet of tin-plated zinc
Plasterboard
Masking tape
A nail punch
A hammer
Protective goggles
A drill with a small metal bit
Tin snips
An old bottle
A pop rivet gun
Disposable gloves
Haematite
A saucer
Cotton wool balls
Wire wool

Lay the tracing paper horizontally. Using the template on page 153, trace the design for the punched tin lantern. Using a permanent pen, mark out a scallop design along one long edge of the tin-plated zinc. Secure the zinc to a piece of plasterboard with masking tape; then lay the tracing paper over the zinc and tape this down.

Position the nail punch over the outline of the pencilled design and hammer it in sharp strong strokes to make an indentation in the tin. Move the nail punch approximately 5mm (¼in) along the outline and punch another indentation. Continue until you have punched indentations along the entire design. Remove the tracing paper.

Wearing protective goggles, use a drill with a small metal bit to drill through each punched indentation into the plasterboard beneath, taking care not to drill through the plasterboard. Continue until the entire design is drilled. Remove the zinc from the plasterboard and dust off any metal shavings.

Using tin snips, cut out the scallop shapes along the top of the zinc. Then wrap the zinc around an old bottle to shape it, overlapping

the edges by 2cm (¾in). Where the zinc overlaps, mark two points with a permanent pen. Secure the lantern together at these two points using a pop rivet gun.

Next, wearing disposable gloves, dip a cotton wool ball into haematite and wipe it over the lantern to age the metal; the haematite will react with the zinc to turn it black. Wet a pad of wire wool and rub this over the lantern; this will remove most of the black, leaving a grey all-over tone with black in areas of detail.

covered lampshade (page 29)

You will need:
An iron
1m (1⅛yd) cotton curtain fabric, 140cm (56in) wide
Adhesive craft spray
A 32cm (13in) lampshade, 25cm (10in) diameter at top, 32cm (13in) diameter at base
Scissors
PVA glue
A 1.5cm (½in) flat fitch brush

Iron the fabric and lay it face down on a flat surface. Spray a thin coat of adhesive craft spray over both the fabric and the lampshade. Line up the seam of the lampshade against the edge of the fabric. Roll the shade over the fabric to attach it. Smooth the fabric down to prevent creases. When you reach the seam, allow an extra 2.5cm (1in) of fabric for an overlap. Trim the fabric at the top and bottom of the shade, allowing an extra 2.5cm (1in) for turning.

Turn over the excess fabric at the seam and secure by brushing some PVA glue on the underside. At the top and bottom of the shade, turn the fabric under to the inside and tuck it under the metal frame. Brush a little PVA glue on the inside of the shade and stick the fabric down. Allow to dry for one hour.

bamboo lamp (page 21)

You will need:

- A drill with a 2cm (¾in) spade bit
- A 34cm (14in) disc of MDF, 18mm (¾in) wide
- A 10cm (4in) disc of MDF, 18mm (¾in) wide
- A chisel
- Three 1.5m (5ft) lengths of solid bamboo, 30-34mm (1¼-1½in) wide
- 3m (3¼yd) black cord
- A saw
- Screws, 4cm (1½in) long
- A screwdriver
- A 60cm (2ft) length of hollow bamboo, 30-34 mm (1¼-1½in) wide
- A tape measure
- A light fitting with 3m (3¼yd) flex
- A stapler and staples
- Eggshell paint: black
- A 2.5cm (1in) household paintbrush
- A screw hook
- A paper Chinese lantern

Drill a 2cm (¾in) diameter hole in the centre of each disc of MDF. On the larger disc, chisel out a channel for the light fitting flex from the central hole to the edge.

Lay the three long pieces of bamboo together, and bind them to hold temporarily. Saw the top of the poles at a 35° angle to make a sloping top. Screw the bamboo poles together at three points down their length to secure.

Drill a 1cm (⅜in) wide hole in the smaller hollow piece of bamboo, 25cm (10in) from one end. Remove the plug from the end of the light fitting flex. Thread the flex in the top end of the short piece of bamboo and out through the drilled hole. Then thread it through the small MDF disc, down through the centre of the bound pieces of bamboo, and the large MDF disc. Secure this disc to the main bamboo poles with screws; repeat to attach the small disc to the top of the bamboo poles. Then attach the short piece of bamboo to the bound lengths with two more screws. Replace the plug on the light fitting flex.

Wind black cord around the screws in the main bamboo poles to hide them, and secure with staples. Paint the discs with black eggshell paint and allow to dry. Insert a screw hook in the end of the short piece of bamboo, and hang a paper Chinese lantern from this hook.

parchment lampshade (page 29)

You will need:

- An old conical lampshade, 34cm (14in) long
- 1m (1⅛yd) cream handmade paper
- A pencil
- Scissors
- PVA glue
- 1.5cm (⅝in) flat paintbrush
- 2 pegs

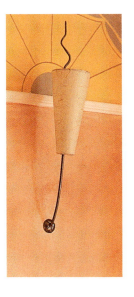

Carefully remove the old paper from the lampshade to use as a template. Place this on the handmade paper and draw around it, allowing an extra 1.5cm (⅝in) all round for turning. Cut out the paper. Bring one long side of the paper over to the other and secure the edges with PVA glue to form a conical shape; hold the glued paper with pegs at each end and allow to dry.

Drop the bottom ring of the lampshade into the cone and hold it 1.5cm (⅝in) up from the bottom. Wrap the paper over the ring to hold it and secure in place with PVA glue; allow to dry. Repeat for the top ring of the shade to complete the shade.

DECORATIVE PROJECTS 107

page 44   page 64

printed tablecloth (page 48)

You will need:
- A sewing machine
- Matching sewing thread
- 2m (2¼yd) Irish linen, 135cm (54in) wide
- Copyright-free source books
- Scissors
- Baking foil
- Image transfer solution
- A paintbrush
- Paper towels
- A sponge

Using a sewing machine threaded with sewing thread to match the linen fabric, stitch a roll hem around the edges of the linen to prepare the tablecloth. Lay the cloth over a flat surface. Select the images to be transferred to the tablecloth from a copyright-free source book. Photocopy as many as required.

Transferring the images

Cut out each image and place them one at a time printed-side up on a sheet of baking foil. Squeeze a generous amount of image transfer solution on to the image and, using a clean paintbrush, spread the paste over the entire surface. Then carefully pick up the wet print and place it on the fabric, paste-side down, flattening it down and blotting excess solution with a scrunched-up paper towel. Repeat with each image to be transferred. Leave to dry for four hours or preferably overnight.

When dry, dab a wet sponge over each paper cut-out and peel it off the fabric, rubbing with the sponge until all the bits of paper are removed. The images will now be printed on to the tablecloth. Leave to dry thoroughly. Paint a further thin coat of image transfer solution over each image to seal and prevent the ink from running. Leave to dry overnight.

picture bow (page 68)

You will need:
- 1m (1⅛yd) ribbon
- Scissors
- A tape measure
- An iron (optional)
- A needle
- Matching sewing thread
- A stapler and staples
- A picture hook or panel pin
- A hammer

Cut a length of ribbon 82cm (33in) long and tie a bow to suit the size of the picture. Fold it out neatly, trim the ends and press the bow if required. Cut another length of ribbon approximately 60cm (24in) long and fold it in half. Stitch this ribbon on to the back of the bow at the crease point; this should be done very securely as it has to take the weight of your picture. Turn over the picture and staple the ends of the folded ribbon on to the frame – one staple should be sufficient. Attach the bow to the wall with a small picture hook or panel pin.

108 THE PROJECTS

These smart picture bows (page 68), cheerful gingham lampshade (page 68) and ticking bolster (page 68) are some of the accessories in the Swedish bedroom.

DECORATIVE PROJECTS

page 36 page 84 page 84 page 78

canvas artwork (page 43)

You will need:
A ready-stretched canvas on a frame
A pencil
A set square or long ruler
Emulsion paint: orange, red
A 2.5cm (1in) household paintbrush
Low-tack masking tape

This project was made using a standard A2 size of canvas. Make light pencil marks along the bottom of the canvas where you want the lines to start; work freehand and judge the pattern by eye for the most spontaneous results. Using the set square or long ruler, extend the pencil lines up to the top of the canvas, being careful to keep the lines exactly vertical. (If you don't have a set square, mark a second set of pencil marks along the top of the canvas using a ruler to make sure that they correspond exactly with those at the bottom,
then simply join the dots together.)

Paint over the canvas with orange emulsion. You should still be able to see your pencil lines faintly through the paint. When dry, mask off alternate lines and paint the stripe between with red emulsion. Apply a second coat if necessary; when dry, remove the tape. For a subtler result, use two paints of the same colour, one in a matt and the other in a gloss finish.

jewelled cross (page 89)

You will need:
A pencil
Tracing paper
45cm (18in) square of MDF 18mm (¾in) thick
A workmate and a jigsaw
A protective face mask
Medium-grade sandpaper
Emulsion paint: ultramarine
PVA glue
A 5cm (2in) household paintbrush
Glass nuggets in assorted colours
Tile grout
A flexible spreader
A sponge
A length of cord
2 screw eyes
A picture hook and nail
A hammer

Enlarge the template on page 151, and transfer this to a piece of MDF using tracing paper and a pencil. Clamp the MDF in a workmate. Wearing a protective face mask, cut out the cross shape using a jigsaw. Sand off any rough edges with sandpaper. Paint the sides of the cross and 1cm (½in) around the front edges with ultramarine emulsion paint. Allow the paint to dry for at least two hours.

Using PVA glue, stick coloured glass nuggets over the front of the cross to cover it completely, and allow to dry overnight. Spread tile grout over the nuggets with a flexible spreader, pushing it into the gaps with your fingers. Wipe excess grout away from the cross with a dampened sponge until the nuggets are shiny. Allow to dry.

Attach a length of cord across the back of the jewelled cross using screw eyes, and nail a picture hook to the wall. To hang the cross, simply hang the cord on the hook.

110 THE PROJECTS

pewter-covered mirror frame (page 88)

You will need:
- Plain, chunky, square-framed mirror frame
- A tape measure
- Sheets of thin-gauge pewter
- A cutting mat
- A stanley knife
- A 5 x 2.5cm (2 x 1in) smooth-edged batten
- Epoxy resin glue
- Small copper-headed nails
- A tack hammer
- Disposable gloves
- Haematite
- A saucer
- Cotton wool balls
- Wire wool

Remove the glass from the mirror. Measure the frame and work out how many panels of pewter you will need to cover it, and how large each panel should be. For this frame, which measures 70cm (28in) square, 20 panels were used, each 20cm (8in) square.

Place a sheet of pewter on a cutting mat and cut out the panels with a stanley knife. Spread epoxy resin over a small area of the mirror frame, front and sides, and over one panel of pewter. Working quickly, lay the glued panel over the glued area of the mirror frame, pressing it down with the smooth edge of the batten; fold the pewter neatly round the frame to the back. Then repeat the process to apply the next panel, overlapping it over the first by 6mm (¼in). Continue to cover the entire frame with pewter. When you come to a corner, cut and fold the pewter as required.

When the whole frame is covered, smooth it down again with the batten. Where the pieces overlap, hammer in small copper-headed nails, 1.5cm (½in) apart, for added detail.

Wearing disposable gloves, dip a cotton wool ball into haematite. Rub this over the surface of the pewter; the haematite will corrode the metal and you will see it turn black.

Dip a pad of wire wool into some water; rub this over the surface to remove most of the black, leaving a lightly tarnished surface with black details. When dry, replace the mirror glass in the frame.

silvered mirror frame (page 82)

You will need:
- A moulded mirror frame
- Masking tape (optional)
- White acrylic primer
- Two 2.5cm (1in) household paintbrushes
- Emulsion paint: lilac
- Acrylic water-based size
- A soft brush
- 30 aluminium leaves, 15 x 15cm (6 x 6 in) (loose in paper)
- A tray
- Wire wool
- Methylated spirits
- Clear button polish and a cloth

Remove the mirror from the frame if possible, but if not mask off the glass. Apply a coat of white acrylic primer over the frame and allow to dry, then paint on two coats of lilac emulsion, allowing two hours' drying time between each coat.

Then paint on a thin, even coat of water-based size, avoiding bubbles. Leave to dry for 15 to 20 minutes when it should be clear and tacky.

Carefully lay the aluminium leaf over the size, and smooth over the surface using your fingers and a soft brush to push it into any areas of detail and to smooth off any excess. Do this over a tray so that you can catch any bits and pieces; use these to fill in any gaps. Continue until the surface is covered.

Dip some wire wool into methylated spirits and wipe it over the surface to remove some of the leaf and reveal some of the lilac base coat. Be careful not to rub too hard. Allow to dry, then paint on a thin, even coat of button polish to seal. Dry for 30 minutes. Mix a little lilac emulsion with water. Brush this all over the surface, then quickly take off any excess with a cloth. This will give an aged look with crusty lilac in the mouldings. Allow to dry.

page 70   page 78   page 24   page 24

display niche (page 76)

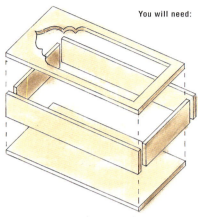

You will need:

- A pencil
- Tracing paper
- A sheet of rough sawn softwood, approximately 1m (1⅓yd) square and 12mm (½in) thick
- A workmate
- A protective face mask
- A jigsaw
- Coarse-grade sandpaper
- Wood glue
- Screws, 3.5cm (1½in) long
- A screwdriver
- White acrylic wood primer
- 5cm (2in) household paintbrushes
- Emulsion paint: ochre, terracotta
- A 1.5cm (½in) fitch brush
- Antique pine tinted varnish
- Gold gilt cream
- A selection of Indian artefacts and trinkets
- Epoxy resin glue
- Burnt umber artist's acrylic colour

Enlarge the template (page 152) and transfer the shape on to a piece of softwood measuring 67 x 42cm (27 x 17in). Mark out all the remaining pieces of the niche on the soft wood, following the diagram. Clamp the wood in a workmate and, wearing a protective face mask, cut out the shapes with a jigsaw. Smooth down any rough edges with coarse-grade sandpaper.

Attach the sides of the box together using wood glue and screws. Then lay them on a flat surface and place the back over the top; attach with wood glue and screws. Turn the box over and place the front of the niche over the top; again, attach with wood glue and screws. Allow the box to dry for two hours.

Apply a coat of acrylic wood primer over the entire box, and allow to dry for one to two hours. Then apply a coat of ochre emulsion to the inside of the box and leave to dry for two to three hours. Next, paint two coats of terracotta emulsion on the outside of the box, allowing each coat to dry for two to three hours before applying the next.

When dry, dip the tip of a fitch brush into tinted varnish and dry-brush the inside and outside of the box in the direction of the woodgrain. Using your finger, apply gilt cream to the edges of the front of the display niche.

Lay out your selection of Indian artefacts on a table and work out the position of each item within the niche. Stick the objects in the niche with epoxy resin and allow to dry thoroughly. To give extra depth to the niche, dry-brush some burnt umber on to and around the objects.

chrome-effect cafe table (page 82)

You will need:

- A protective face mask
- A small table
- A dust sheet
- Grey car spray primer
- Chrome car spray
- Spray lacquer

Work outside or in a well-ventilated area, and wear a face mask to protect against inhalation of the paint. Place the table on a dust sheet. Shake the can of grey car spray primer well and, holding it 30cm (12in) away from the surface, work in sweeping movements to spray the table with an even coating. Dry for 30 minutes.

Shake the can of chrome car spray well, then spray two to three coats over the primed surface. Work in sweeping movements as before to maintain an even coverage. Allow to dry for 30 minutes, then spray on a coat of the lacquer following the same spraying technique, to seal.

terracotta-effect urn (page 28)

You will need:
White acrylic primer
A 5cm (2in) household paintbrush
An urn
Emulsion paint: peach, white
Old cloths or towels
Round fitch brushes
A plant mister
Acrylic matt varnish (optional)
A varnish brush (optional)

Ensure that the urn is free from dust and grease. Then paint a coat of white acrylic primer all over the surface of the urn and allow to dry for at least one hour. Next, apply two coats of peach emulsion over the urn, allowing two to three hours' drying time between each coat of paint.

Stand the urn on some old cloths or towels to protect the underlying surface. Ensure the urn is vertical so that any drips roll downwards as they would do in natural terracotta. Dilute the peach emulsion with an equal quantity of water. Dab on some of this mix at the top of the urn with a fitch brush and spray water over it using a plant mister so that the peach paint dribbles down the sides of the urn.

Build up the effect by dabbing some diluted white paint on to the top of the urn with the fitch brush, then spraying on some more water so that more dribbles drip down the sides. Continue to apply dilute paint around the rim of the urn and spray it with water until the desired effect is achieved. Allow to dry. Seal the surface with two coats of acrylic matt varnish, if desired, allowing the first coat to dry before applying the second.

urn firescreen (page 28)

You will need:
Tracing paper
A pencil
1.5m (5ft) MDF, 12mm (½in) thick
A jigsaw
Medium-grade sandpaper
A ruler
45 x 10cm (18 x 4in) piece of MDF, 18mm (¾in) thick
Two 30cm (12in) lengths of batten, 5 x 2.5cm (2 x 1in)
A hammer
Nails, 2.5cm (1in) long
White acrylic primer
2.5cm (1in) and 5cm (2in) household paintbrushes
Emulsion paint: grey-brown, pale yellow, deep yellow, pale brown, dark brown
Acrylic gold paint
Assorted artist's brushes
Acrylic matt varnish
A varnish brush

Enlarge the urn template (page 153), and transfer it on to the thin MDF. Cut out the shape with a jigsaw and sand the rough edges. Mark a centre line horizontally across the piece of thick MDF. Mark two more lines, each 6mm (¼in) from the central line on each side. Attach a batten up to each outer line using a hammer and nails. Sit the urn in the slit and secure it with nails hammered through the batten at each side.

Prime the screen with a coat of acrylic primer. Paint two coats of grey-brown emulsion over the urn, excluding the plinth; allow to dry. Using an urn as a guide, paint in the highlights on the urn screen with shades of yellow paint. Then, using darker brown tones, fill in the shadows. When dry, paint the plinth gold, and apply two coats of matt varnish over the urn to seal.

page 24 page 10 page 56 page 56

column pedestal (page 26)

You will need:
- 45cm (18in) square of MDF 32mm (1¼in) thick
- Wire cutters
- Chicken wire
- A tape measure
- Hook tacks
- A hammer
- 45cm (18in) square of MDF 18mm (¾in) thick
- Newspaper and a bucket
- Wallpaper paste
- A hand blender
- Scissors
- 2m (2¼yd) rope
- Nails, 4cm (1½in) long
- Powder filler
- Four 5cm (2in) household paintbrushes
- White acrylic primer
- Emulsion paint: cream, white
- Raw sienna artist's oil colour

Lay the square of thick MDF on a flat surface. Using wire cutters, cut a length of chicken wire 87cm (35in) wide. Fold it in half lengthways, then roll it up to make a column 22cm (9in) in diameter. Trim off excess chicken wire. Turn in the cut edges of the wire, bending them round to secure. Attach the wire column to the square MDF base by hammering in hook tacks around the base. Turn the column upside-down and attach the wire to the thinner MDF top in the same way.

Shred a broadsheet newspaper and put the pieces in a bucket. Add 1.1 litres (2 pints) water and 300g (10½oz) wallpaper paste, then, using a hand blender, blend the mixture to a pulp. Add more water a little at a time, if necessary. Build up the column by pressing the paper pulp into the chicken wire, making ridges in the sides, and smoothing the pulp continually. Allow to dry for at least two days.

Cut a length of rope and place it around the base of the column 5cm (2in) from the chicken wire. Secure it to the base with nails.

Next make two wire sausages 45cm (18in) long and 15cm (6in) in diameter for the top of the column. Coat these with pulp, again forming ridges. Allow to dry for up to two days. Attach these shapes to each side of the column top by hammering nails through the MDF top into each shape. Cut two lengths of rope, each 70cm (28in) long, and attach these to the top of the column, curling from one wire shape to the other; attach them securely with nails.

Make up a thin, washy mix of filler and paint this over the entire surface of the column. Allow to dry for two hours. Paint on a base coat of white acrylic primer, then apply a coat of cream emulsion, allowing each coat to dry before applying the next. Dry-brush white emulsion over the column with random strokes, then dry-brush some raw sienna in the areas of detail to give a sandstone effect. Allow to dry.

shell strings (page 13)

You will need:
- Approximately 10 assorted shells
- A pencil
- A G-clamp
- A small modelling drill
- Approximately 1.5m (5ft) of thick cotton
- Scissors

Choose a variety of shells which are not too thin. Work out the easiest place to drill a hole in each shell and mark this with a pencil. Clamp one shell at a time in a G-clamp. Carefully drill a small hole through the shell using a modelling drill. Repeat to drill holes through about 10 shells.

Take a length of thick cotton and double it, then knot it to create a loop. Thread a shell on to the cotton and tie a knot to secure. Leave a gap of

approximately 15cm (6in), then thread on another shell, again knotting it to secure. Repeat to create a string of shells which can be hung from the top loop of the cotton. Trim away any excess cotton.

woven paper bowl (page 62)

You will need:

Sheet of corrugated card, 1m x 40cm (40 x 16in)
Brightly coloured water-based paints
Artist's paintbrushes
A craft knife
A cutting mat
A ruler and a pencil
Tracing paper
Ticket or very thin card
Bulldog clips
A bowl
A stapler and staples
Scissors
A leather needle
Hemp string
Satin acrylic varnish
A varnish brush

Paint the corrugated card with the brightly coloured paints and leave to dry. Using a craft knife, cut the cardboard across the corrugations into nine strips measuring 5 x 100cm (2 x 40in).

Set aside one strip for the rim and cut the rest in half widthways. Enlarge the template (page 153) so that it measures 45 x 4.5cm (18 x 1¾in). Transfer it on to ticket card. Draw round this template on all 16 strips and cut to size; the shape of the strips will help the basket curve upwards.

Start weaving by folding two strips in half widthways. Make a mark on the folded edge of each. Then unfold the strips and lay one across the other at right angles with the fold marks aligning with the strip edges – this marks the centre. Weave strips under and over alternate strips until you have eight strips in each direction. Hold any edges with bulldog clips.

Insert a bowl in the woven bowl and mark a line around the top edge of the weaving. Staple 1.5cm (⅝in) down from the line all around the bowl and trim. Bend the rim piece in half lengthways, fold it over the edge and sew into place using a leather needle and hemp string. Seal the basket with two to three coats of varnish.

metal fruit bowl (page 62)

You will need:

A large empty olive oil can
A tape measure
A permanent pen
Tin snips
Pliers
A 6mm (¼in) pop rivet gun

Measure 11cm (4½in) up from the bottom of the olive oil can and mark a line around the can with a permanent pen. Carefully cut along the marked line with tin snips. Make one 1.5cm (⅝in) snip downwards from the cut rim and, using the pliers, bend the edge over by 1.5cm (⅝in) all the way around the rim.

With the remainder of the tin, mark out four petal shapes. Cut them out with tin snips, then place them equally around the rim, printed side facing upwards. Bend the petals over the rim as before, and mould the bottom of each petal inside the can to follow the actual shape of the can. Secure each petal into place on the inside of the can using the pop rivet gun: two rivets should be enough for each.

Then cut out four leaf shapes from the spare tin. Position these around the rim, between the petals, with their unprinted side facing upwards. Bend over the edges to the underside as before. Secure in place with the pop rivet gun as before. Finally, ensure there are no jagged pieces of metal sticking out awkwardly which might cause an accident.

DECORATIVE PROJECTS **115**

page 70

soft furnishing projects

These tasselled cushions made from brightly coloured saris (page 74) make sumptuous furnishings in the Indian bedroom.

tasselled sari cushions (page 74)

You will need:
Scissors
Thin hemp string
A tape measure
Gold spray paint
Tracing paper
A pencil
Cotton lining fabric
A sewing machine
Matching thread
Polyester wadding
A sari
Piping cord and pins

These tasselled sari cushions are made with a basic back vent opening, as this is good for lightweight decorative fabrics, providing a quick finish and enabling the inner cover to be removed easily.

Making the tassels

For each one, cut a 10cm (4in) length of hemp string and lay it flat. Then cut 30 lengths of hemp, each 18cm (7in) long. Lay the lengths side by side across the single length of hemp so it is in the centre. Take each end of the single length and carefully tie the ends together in a knot, securing the other lengths. Holding the knotted length in one hand, fold down the long lengths of hemp with your other hand to form the basis of the tassel. Now wind a 15cm (6in) length of hemp around the folded lengths, about 2.5cm (1in) down from the knotted top. Tie off and trim. Spray the tassel all over with gold spray paint, and leave to dry.

Making the cushion

You will need to make an inner cushion as it is impossible to find a pillow pad this shape! Enlarge the template (page 154) and transfer it on to tracing paper. Using this as a pattern, cut out two pieces of cotton lining fabric to make an inner cushion. Sew the two pieces together around three sides. Turn the cover the right way out, insert polyester wadding, then sew up the open edge.

To make the outer cushion cover, cut out a front piece from a sari using the template as above. Cut out two back pieces, each just over half the size of the template. Hem each back piece along one edge which will form the centre back of the cushion. With right sides together, pin the back pieces to the front piece, overlapping the hemmed centre edges, and sandwiching a tassel in each corner so that the knotted end aligns with the corner and the threads of the tassel are pointing towards the centre of the cushion. Stitch around all four sides, taking a 1.5cm (½in) seam. Turn the cover to the right side through the back vent and insert the inner cushion; the two halves of the back will lie together as if closed without further fastening.

To add piping, measure all around the cushion; cut a length of narrow piping cord this length. Cover the cord with your chosen fabric cut into strips on the bias (page 119). To do this, you may need to join the fabrics to get the length you require. Lay the cord on to the fabric; fold the fabric over the cord and stitch close to the cord. Trim the edges. When making the cushion, insert the covered cord between the back and front pieces, positioning the cord on the inside of the seam line. When you sew up the cushion and turn the cover the right way out, the piping will be visible around the edges.

page 10   page 16   page 64

bunting cushion (page 14)

You will need:

56 x 28cm (22 x 11in) cotton canvas
Scissors
Tailor's chalk
28cm (11in) square of striped cotton fabric
A sewing machine
Matching sewing thread
Pins
A cushion pad, 25cm (10in) square
A needle

Cut two squares from the canvas, each measuring 28cm (11in). Using tailor's chalk, mark a triangle on the striped fabric so that the top short edge measures 25cm (10in), and the point of the triangle is 28cm (11in) away from the centre of the top edge. Cut out the triangle. Using a sewing machine threaded with matching thread, zigzag stitch the edges of the triangle to prevent them fraying.

To assemble the cushion cover, lay one piece of canvas down, right side facing, and then lay the triangle right side down on top of it so that the short edge is aligned with the edge of the canvas. Lay the second canvas square on top and pin the fabric layers together around all four edges, ensuring that the point of the triangle is left free. Taking a 1.5cm (½in) seam, stitch around the edges of the fabric layers, leaving a 15cm (6in) gap on one side. Turn the cover the right way out through the gap, then iron the cover. Insert a cushion pad through the gap, pin together the open edge and slipstitch to close. The cushion, complete with flapping bunting, is now ready to be used.

patched silk cushion (page 21)

You will need:

Remnants of Chinese silk, plain and patterned
Scissors
A tape measure
Pins
A sewing machine
Matching sewing thread
An iron
50cm (20in) red velvet, 140cm (56in) wide
Polyester wadding
A needle

Cut out three rectangles measuring 18 x 28cm (7 x 11in), two from plain silk and one from highly patterned Chinese silk. Lay the pieces right side down with the two plain pieces at either side of the patterned one, and pin them together. Sew the pieces together and iron the seams flat.

Cut out a piece of velvet measuring 47 x 28cm (19 x 11in) and lay it right side up. Lay the patched piece right side down over the velvet and pin into place. Sew round the two long sides and one of the short sides. Then turn right side out and iron flat. Stuff the cushion cover with polyester wadding. Then turn in the rough unsewn edges and pin. Slipstitch to close the open edges as neatly as possible.

bolster cushion (page 68)

You will need:
- A tape measure
- A bolster pad
- Striped cotton fabric
- Scissors
- Piping cord
- Pins
- A sewing machine
- Matching sewing thread
- An iron
- A needle
- 2 self-covering buttons (available in kit form)

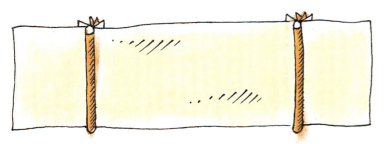

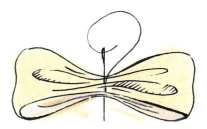

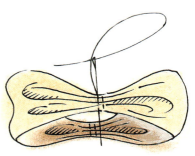

Measure the length and circumference of the bolster pad. Add 1.5cm (½in) extra to each of these measurements to allow for seams. Cut out a piece of fabric following these measurements. Then measure the radius of the bolster end. Cut out two strips of fabric the length of the circumference of the bolster pad and as wide as the radius of the bolster end, again adding an extra 1.5cm (½in) to each measurement.

Cut out two pieces of piping cord equal to the circumference of the bolster pad. Cover the piping cord with fabric, stitching close to the cord. With right sides together and raw edges matching, machine-stitch one of the strips of fabric to one short edge of the main fabric, taking a 1.5cm (½in) seam and sandwiching a length of piping in between the two fabrics. Repeat to attach the remaining piping and fabric strip to the opposite short edge of the main fabric.

Fold the fabric in half lengthways, right sides together, ensuring that the ends of the piping meet each other. Taking a 1.5cm (½in) seam, stitch the long edges of the fabric together to make a tube. Turn the fabric the right way out and press.

Insert the bolster pad into the part-finished cover. The piped edges should sit at the edge of each end of the bolster. Turn in the raw edges at each bolster end to meet in the centre of the circle. Then, either gather or pleat the fabric by stitching a double row of running stitches in the centre of each end. Secure by oversewing into place.

Making a maltese cross

To cover the bolster ends and hide the overlapping fabric, you can make a maltese cross to add a finishing touch. To do this, first measure the diameter of the bolster end. Cut two strips of fabric which are twice the diameter of the bolster end and 20cm (8in) wide. Fold the strips in half lengthwise, right sides together, and machine stitch along the long edge, taking a 1.5cm (½in) seam. Turn the strips the right way out, move the seam to the centre of each strip and press flat. Bring the two short ends of the strip together, with the seam on the inside, slip one short end of the strip into the other to make a ring. Stitch the ends together with zigzag stitch. Repeat with the second strip.

Take one of the rings and flatten it with the zigzagged seam at the centre back. Pinch the centre together into little pleats to make a bow shape. Sew these pleats into place, so the front of the bow is stitched to the back. Repeat with the second ring, but this time pleating each side separately, so it still remains a ring.

Slip the bow inside the second ring to form a cross shape, and stitch them together at the centre of the cross. Cover a self-covering button with matching fabric by cutting a piece of fabric slightly larger than the button, laying it over the top and tucking the ends under, then snapping the bottom disc into the top to secure the fabric in place. Sew the button to the centre of the cross. Sew the maltese cross on to the end of the bolster with tiny stitches.

Repeat the process to make a second maltese cross for the other end of the bolster.

| page 44 | page 24 | page 78 | page 78 |

cushion with voile pockets (page 46)

You will need:

Images of silhouettes
A tape measure
Scissors
50cm (20in) cream cotton canvas
Adhesive craft spray
50cm (20in) peach cotton voile
Pins and a needle
A sewing machine
Matching sewing thread
50cm (20in) peach brocade
An iron
A cushion pad, 37cm (15in) square

From your own silhouettes or from a copyright-free book, photocopy four silhouettes approximately 12cm (5in) square. Then, instead of cutting them out, rip the edges for a more natural effect.

Next, measure and cut out a 40cm (16in) square of cream cotton canvas. Lay the four photocopies in the centre of the canvas to form a square shape, leaving a small space between each. Spray the back of each photocopy sparingly with adhesive craft spray and stick it in place on the fabric.

Cut a piece of peach voile to the same size as the canvas and lay it over the top of the silhouettes. Pin the voile to the canvas around the edges. Using a sewing machine threaded with peach sewing thread stitch a square all around the photocopies to contain them, and then stitch a line running from centre top to centre bottom, and another line from one centre side to the other, to divide the silhouettes.

Lay the finished piece canvas-side down on to a piece of peach brocade and cut the brocade to size. Pin the layers of fabric together and machine stitch around the edges taking a 1.5cm (½in) seam. Leave a gap at one side of the cover. Turn the cover the right way out through the gap; iron it with a cool iron. Insert a cushion pad, pin the edges of the gap together and slipstitch the open edge to close.

fringed cushion (page 29)

You will need:

Scissors
A tape measure
1m (1⅛yd) urn-patterned fabric, 150cm (60in) wide
1m (1⅛yd) linen union
A sewing machine
Matching sewing thread
Pins
An iron
A needle and a button
A 40cm (16in) square cushion pad
1.5m (5ft) fringing

Cut out a 42cm (17in) square from the urn fabric. Cut out two back pieces from linen union, each measuring 42 x 24cm (17 x 9½in). Hem each piece along one long edge. With right sides facing, pin the back pieces to the front piece, so the hemmed edges are in the centre. Sew around all sides, taking a 1.5cm (½in) seam. Turn the cover the right way out and iron. Sew a button to the back vent for decoration. Insert the cushion pad. Cut a length of fringe 161cm (64½in) long. Pin the fringe around the edge of the reverse of the cushion. Carefully handstitch into place.

lined curtains (page 81)

You will need:
- A tape measure
- Scissors
- 17m (18½yd) patterned slub silk, 140cm (56in) wide
- 17m (18½yd) lining fabric, 140cm (56in) wide
- Pins
- A sewing machine
- Matching sewing thread
- An iron
- 4m (4⅓yd) cotton triple rufflette tape, 7cm (3in) wide
- Curtain hooks
- A curtain track

These materials are sufficient to make two curtains for a window measuring 278 x 133cm (111 x 53in). To make curtains for a larger or smaller window, adjust the measurements accordingly.

Measure your window, adding 62cm (25in) to the length and multiplying the width by 1½; this is the amount of fabric you need. Cut out the fabric. For this window, this involved cutting four strips of 3.5m (3⅞yd) fabric at full width and then a fifth strip which was cut in half lengthways. Cut out the same amount of lining fabric.

Making the curtain

Lay out the main fabric and pin together lengthways two strips and one half strip for each curtain. Sew the lengths together, remove the pins, and press. Turn in a 6cm (2½in) hem at the sides, iron and sew. Turn over a hem of 25cm (10in) at the bottom and iron, pin and sew. Turn over the top by 36cm (15in) and cut off any excess. Pin and sew 2cm (¾in) from the top.

Repeat for the lining fabric: turn in a 12cm (5in) hem at the sides, iron, pin and sew. Turn under a 15cm (6in) hem at the bottom, then iron, pin and sew. Turn over the top by 16cm (6¼in) and cut off any excess. Pin, iron and sew 2cm (¾in) from the top. Lay the main fabric and lining together, wrong sides facing, and top edges matching; ensure that the shorter sides are an equal distance away from each side; the lining should be slightly shorter than the curtain fabric at the bottom. Pin together and handstitch up both sides.

Attach the rufflette tape to the top of the curtain, on the lining side. Trim off any excess and fold the ends under. Sew in place along the top and bottom of the tape. Pull out the strings and knot at one end. Pull the tape up to the required width and knot. Attach the curtain hooks on to the tape and hang the curtain from the track.

stamped voile curtains (page 81)

You will need:
- 12m (12¾yd) voile, 140cm (56in) wide
- Scissors
- Emulsion paint: white
- A cloth and a board
- A cork
- A tape measure
- An iron and pins
- Matching sewing thread
- A sewing machine
- Curtain wire
- Tin snips or pliers
- 4 screw eyes
- 8 screw hooks

Cut the voile into four 3m (3¼yd) lengths. Pour some white emulsion into a saucer. Lay a clean cloth on to a board to absorb any excess paint, then lay a length of voile on top. Dip the end of a cork into the paint, and stamp it on a piece of paper to test it. Then dip the cork in the paint again and stamp it on to the voile. Repeat to decorate all four strips of voile.

When dry, trim the voile pieces to fit the length of the window; here each piece was trimmed to 288cm (3yd). The side edges of the voile can be left as they are. Make a roll hem at the base of the voile pieces by turning under 4cm (1½in), then ironing and pinning in place. At the top of each piece, make a roll hem of 8cm (3¼in), iron and pin. Sew the top and bottom hems with matching thread and remove the pins. At the top of each piece of voile, sew another line of stitches 1cm (⅜in) down from the top, then another line 2cm (¾in) down.

Measure the width of the window. Cut the curtain wire 10cm (4in) shorter using tin snips or pliers. Then cut this piece of wire into four equal-sized pieces. Attach four screw eyes along the top of the window frame, two at each side and two spaced equally between, then screw hooks to each end of the curtain wire lengths. Thread one piece of wire through the channel at the top of each voile curtain. Hook each end over the screw eyes to hang the curtains.

SOFT FURNISHING PROJECTS **121**

page 16   page 24

banner curtains and tie blind (page 21)

You will need:

Scissors
A tape measure
10m (12yd) parchment-coloured silk, 140cm (56in) wide
6.5m (7¼yd) interlining, 140cm (56in) wide
6.5m (7¼yd) black lining fabric, 140cm (56in) wide
8m (8½yd) highly coloured black Chinese silk, 140cm (56in) wide
Pins
A sewing machine
Matching sewing thread
An iron
A needle
2m (2¼yd) rufflette tape, 7cm (3in) deep
2m (2¼yd) touch-and-close tape, 7cm (3in) wide
6m (6½yd) cream muslin, 3.3m (3½yd) wide
6.5m (7¼yd) black cotton, 140cm (56in) wide
197cm (79in) dowel, 2mm (⅟₁₆in) thick
4 nails, 2.5cm (1in) long
A hammer
A 1.8 x 1.2m (8 x 4ft) sheet of MDF, 9mm (⅜in) thick
A pencil
A workmate and a saw
Lengths of 5 x 2.5cm (2 x 1in) batten
Screws, 2.5cm (1in) long
A screwdriver
Woodfiller
Medium-grade sandpaper
A stapler and staples
2 angle brackets, 12 x 10cm (5 x 4in)
A drill

The measurements given here will make a pair of curtains 3m (3⅓yd) long and 115cm (46in) wide. The border measures 15cm (6in). To make larger or smaller curtains, adjust the measurements accordingly.

Cut out the following pieces of fabric for the curtains: two pieces of parchment silk 90m x 300cm (36in x 116in); two pieces of interlining 115 x 300cm (46 x 120in); two pieces of black lining 120 x 305cm (48 x 122in); four pieces of black silk 20 x 310cm (8 x 124in); and two pieces of black silk 20 x 120cm (8 x 48in).

Making the curtains

Each curtain consists of a central piece of parchment silk framed at the bottom and sides by pieces of black silk. These are then lined with black lining, with interlining sandwiched between the layers.

For detailed instructions on making the curtains, follow the instructions for making the Chinese banner (page 131).

Cut the rufflette tape into two 120cm (48in) pieces. Pin these on to the top of each curtain, turning under 2.5cm (1in) at each end. Stitch carefully to the top of the curtain. Pull the rufflette tape up to 70cm (28in) and knot each end tightly. Measure and cut two pieces of touch-and-close tape 115cm (46in) long. Peel one side off each piece. Sew the hairier side to the top of the curtain with small handstitches.

Making the blind

This window measured 197cm (79in) square but 50cm (20in) was added to the length of the blind so that it reached the floor. To make a blind for a smaller or larger window, adjust the measurements.

Measure and cut two pieces of cream muslin measuring 205 x 280cm (82 x 112in). Place them together right sides facing; pin, then sew them together around three sides. Turn right side out through the open edge and iron. Turn in the open edge and pin, then handstitch to close 1cm (½in) from the edge. Stitch a line all the way around the fabric 1cm (½in) from the edge. Turn the top edge over by 3.5cm (1½in). Pin, then sew a line 2.5cm (1in) from the top edge to make a stitched channel.

For the ties, measure and cut out two pieces of black cotton 6.5m (7¼yd) long and 50cm (20in) wide. Fold each in half lengthways, right sides together, and sew all around the edge leaving one short side open. Turn the tie the right way out and iron flat. Handstitch the open edge to close.

Thread the dowel through the channel at the top of the blind. Loop the ties over the blind, 75cm (30in) from each side, roll up the blind and knot the ties at the bottom of the blind to secure. To hang the blind, hammer four nails into the top of the window frame and place the dowel on these.

Making the pelmet

For this window, measuring 197cm (79in) square, the pelmet measured 237cm (95in) long and 60cm (26in) wide.

Mark on to the MDF the following shapes: one front piece measuring 237 x 90cm (95 x 36in) and two side pieces measuring 65 x 20cm (26 x 8in). Secure the MDF in a workmate, and cut the pieces out with a saw. Then saw two pieces measuring 65cm (26in) long. Screw the two small pieces of batten to the edge of the two side pieces. Secure these side pieces to the front of the pelmet by inserting screws through the front of the pelmet into the side pieces. Fill any holes with woodfiller and, when dry, sand off to a flat finish.

To make the structure more secure, attach one length of batten along the top of the pelmet, securing it in place to the front of the pelmet with screws; fill as before. Repeat to attach a second batten along the top of the pelmet and secure at the back with screws as before.

Cut out the following pieces of fabric for the pelmet: a piece of parchment-coloured silk measuring 65cm x 3m (26 x120in), and a piece of black decorated silk measuring 3m x 30cm (120 x 12in). Turn under the edges of the black silk panel and sew it on to the parchment-coloured panel so the long sides are matching. Turn under the edges of the parchment silk panel and iron carefully. Stretch the stitched panel over the front and sides of the pelmet and staple into place on the inside of the pelmet at the back. Stitch the two remaining pieces of touch-and-close tape to the top front of the pelmet and add staples for extra security.

Attach the brackets on the wall and hook the pelmet over. Hang the curtains on the pelmet using the touch-and-close tape.

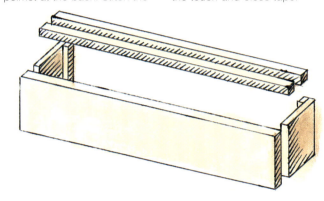

curtains with tabs (page 29)

These materials are sufficient to make two curtains for a bay window measuring 442cm (172in) wide by 288cm (115in) high. If your window is a different size, adjust the materials accordingly.

Each curtain is 110cm (41½in) wide and 270cm (108in) long, excluding the tabs. The folded tabs measure 13cm (5¼in) long.

You will need:
- 20m (21⅞yd) linen union, 150cm (60in) wide
- Scissors
- A tape measure
- 20m (21⅞yd) lining fabric, 150cm (60in) wide
- Pins
- Matching sewing thread
- A sewing machine
- An iron
- Tailor's chalk
- Touch-and-close tape
- 16 suede-covered buttons

Sewing the curtains

For each curtain, cut out a piece of linen measuring 280 x 120cm (112 x 48in); then cut out a piece of lining fabric to match. Turn under the edges of each piece by 5cm (2in) and pin. Lay the linen down right side facing; place the lining on top, right side down. Pin all the way around, allowing a 5cm (2in) turning. Sew the bottom edge and both side edges. Turn right side out through the open edge and iron flat.

Sewing the tabs

Next make up eight tabs for each curtain from the linen. For each tab, cut two pieces of linen measuring 28 x 15cm (11 x 6in). Pin the pieces together, right sides facing. Mark a point in the centre of one short edge. Sew from this point to each long edge, about 5cm (2in) from the end to create a point. Leave the other short edge unstitched. Turn the tab the right side out and iron flat. The finished tab should measure 25 x 12cm (10 x 5in) with a 5cm (2in) tapered point at one end. Repeat to make fifteen more tabs.

Insert the unfinished end of the tabs into the top end of the curtain, folding the curtain edges under. Space the tabs evenly then pin into place. Stitch along the top edge. Fold the tabs over and secure to the curtain with a square of touch-and-close tape, attached to the curtain and the tab. For a decorative finishing touch, sew a suede-covered button to the front of each tab.

page 70   page 10

Driftwood and shells make unusual and apt toggles for the pull-cords of the canvas sail blind (page 14) in the Long Island beach house.

sari curtains (page 72)

You will need:

A sari, approximately 7 x 1m (7¾ x 1⅛yd)
Scissors
A tape measure
7m (7⅝yd) striped Indian cotton, 140cm (56in) wide
An iron
Pins
A sewing machine
Matching sewing thread
A needle

Cut the sari in half lengthways to make two curtains, each 3.5m (3⅞yd) long. Cut the Indian cotton in half lengthways to provide two 3.5m (3⅞yd) lengths. Iron all the fabric.

Lay the pieces of Indian cotton right side up on to the floor; place the sari pieces right side down on top of the cotton. Trim the cotton up to the edges of the sari and pin the two fabrics together for each curtain. Using a sewing machine threaded with matching sewing thread, stitch up the long sides and the top of each curtain, taking a 1.5cm (⅝in) seam, and leaving the bottom edge unstitched. Remove the pins. Turn each curtain inside out and iron carefully on a low setting. Fold in the bottom edge, then pin and slipstitch along the bottom edge to complete.

To hang the curtain, wrap it over the curtain pole a third of the way along the curtain so that the striped underside hangs from the back of the pole and is visible from the room. Pull the front of the curtain to one side of the window and drape it around a curtain stay (page 142).

canvas sail blind (page 14)

You will need:

1.5 x 2m (1⅔ x 2⅛yd) cotton duck canvas, 250g (9oz) weight
Pins and scissors
A sewing machine with a denim needle
Matching strong thread
A pencil
A tape measure
2cm (¾in) brass eyelets
An eyelet punch
5m (6yd) sash window cord
Masking tape
A curtain pole and fixings
2 pieces of driftwood
2 shells
A drill and drill bit

This sail blind will fit a window measuring 190cm (76in) wide by 126cm (51in) high. For a different size window, adjust the amount of canvas accordingly.

Making the blind

Pin a 5cm (2in) hem all around the edge of the canvas. Stitch the hem using a sewing machine fitted with a denim needle, threaded with strong cream thread. Lay the canvas out flat. Mark out with a pencil the eyelet points approximately 15cm (6in) apart within the hem along the top and two sides of the canvas. With small scissors, cut a small hole at each point. Following the instructions on the eyelet punch, fix the eyelets into the canvas.

Threading the cord

Wrap tape around the cut edges of the sash cord to prevent further fraying and to aid threading. Working from the bottom left corner of the canvas, thread the cord in and out of the eyelets until you reach the top left corner. Fix a curtain pole to the wall above the window following the manufacturer's instructions. Attach the blind to the pole by weaving the cord in and out of the eyelets along the top edge of the canvas, at the same time wrapping it over the pole to encase it. Continue weaving the cord through the eyelets until you reach the bottom right edge. Cut off any excess cord and tape the end again.

Securing cord ends

To secure the ends of cord at the bottom sides of the canvas, find two pieces of driftwood. Drill a 1cm (⅜in) hole through each piece and thread one end of the cord through each. Then drill a hole through two shells (shell strings, page 114) and thread one shell on to each cord. Tie a knot in the cord underneath each shell to secure. To pull up the blind, push up the driftwood to the level required and tie a further knot in the cord.

page 84 page 70 page 70 page 24

dyed lace blind (page 89)

You will need:
- A lace tablecloth, larger than the window
- Pink fabric dye
- An iron
- Spray starch
- A tape measure
- A roller blind kit, to fit the window
- A straight edge
- Pins
- Scissors
- A sewing machine or a needle
- Matching sewing thread
- A stapler and staples
- A screwdriver

Wash and dry the lace tablecloth to remove any film or coating. Dye the tablecloth with pink fabric dye, following the manufacturer's instructions. Allow to dry and iron flat. Spray the fabric on both sides with spray starch to stiffen it, then iron again.

Measure the length of the pole in the blind kit. Mark this measurement on the dyed lace using a straight edge and pins. Then measure the height of the window; add 15cm (6in) to this measurement and mark this out on the lace. Cut the blind to size.

Fold the bottom edge of the lace up by 7.5cm (3in) and pin to secure. Turn the ends under and sew a plain running stitch by machine or by hand about 5cm (2in) from the bottom. Thread the batten from the blind kit through this channel. Lay the pole for the blind at the top edge of the lace. Fold over the top edge of the fabric and staple it to the pole, following the instructions given in the kit. Screw the blind attachments into place. Hang the blind at the window.

re-covered chair (page 76)

You will need:
- A claw hammer
- Brown paper
- A pencil
- Scissors
- Cotton wadding, 115g (4oz) weight
- Heavyweight upholstery fabric
- A tack hammer
- A packet of 250 rust-antiqued, dome-headed upholstery studs

Using a claw hammer, remove the old studs and fabric from the chair seat. Retain the old fabric and wadding to make a template for the new covering. To do this, place the old wadding and fabric on a piece of brown paper, draw around both pieces then cut them out. Cut the new wadding to the exact shape of the template. Then cut out the new fabric, adding an extra 2.5cm (1in) all round the edge of the template to allow for turning the raw edges under.

Carefully lay the wadding over the chair and then place the tweed over the top. Fold the excess fabric under to conceal the edges. Using the tack hammer, and checking that the fabric is taut, tap in upholstery studs approximately 1.5cm (½in) apart through the fabric and into the rail of the chair all the way round the seat.

To re-cover the back of the chair, follow the same procedure as above.

126 THE PROJECTS

stamped leather pouffe (page 76)

You will need:
A pouffe
Brown suedette
Gold fabric paint
A saucer
A 2.5cm (1in) household paintbrush
2 paisley-design rubber stamps, 1 large and 1 small
A tea-towel
An iron
Scissors
Strong sewing thread
A leather needle
A sewing machine
Leather sewing machine needle

These materials are sufficient to cover a pouffe measuring 55cm (22in) high by 33cm (13in) wide.

Lay the suedette down flat. Pour some gold fabric paint into a saucer and dip a paintbrush into it. Then paint an even layer of paint over one stamp, ensuring it is entirely covered. Lay the stamp firmly on to the suedette, then lift it off carefully to reveal the stamped design. Repeat the stamping process, working with both the large and small stamps for a varied design. When you have covered the suedette, allow the paint to dry for 30 minutes. To seal the paint, lay the suedette face down and place a tea-towel over the top; using an iron on a low setting, iron over the tea-towel.

Remove the cover from the pouffe and unpick it to provide a template which will have the allowance included. Using this template, cut out the stamped suedette to this shape. Using sewing thread and a leather needle, tack the pieces together before sewing. If there was a zip on the template, leave this open as a vent on the new fabric. Carefully stitch the pieces together using a sewing machine fitted with a leather sewing machine needle.

Place the new cover on the pouffe, tucking the bottom neatly under the base, and securing with small handstitches. Tuck and fold under the open vent and handstitch into place.

linen-covered settee (page 28)

You will need:
190 x 65cm (76 x 26in) foam, 10cm (4in) thick
10m (10⅔yd) linen union, 150cm (60in) wide
Matching sewing thread
A sewing machine and scissors
A pencil and brown paper
An upholstery needle
4 suede-covered buttons
Two 25 x 5cm (10 x 2in) tabs of leather
Strong thread
A leather needle

Cover the settee foam seating as for the day bed (page 148).

Make a template of the settee cover by drawing around the old cover on brown paper. Cut out pieces of linen union following the templates, allowing an extra 2.5cm (1in) all around for stitching. Pin and sew them together following the template.

Lay the stitched fabric over the settee. Pull up the fabric at the front of the arms into a gather and secure with small stitches using an upholstery needle. Sew two buttons to the front of each settee arm and loop a leather tab from one button to the other. Secure the tab in place using strong thread and a leather needle. Repeat with the other arm.

page 36 page 50 page 64 page 70

foam lounger (page 42)

You will need:

High-density foam cube, 1m x 1m x 50cm (1¼yd x 1¼yd x 20in)
6m (6½yd) art felt, 182cm (71in) wide
Tailor's chalk
A tape measure
Scissors
Pins
Foam mount upholstery adhesive
A needle and matching sewing thread (optional)

Order your foam cube from specialist cutters, who will be able to supply you with any dimension you require. If you would prefer a smaller cube, adjust the materials accordingly.

Lay out the felt on a flat surface and mark and cut out two squares to fit exactly the top and bottom of the foam cube. It should be possible to cover the remaining sides of the cube with just one piece of felt. Cut this third piece deep enough to cover the depth of the cube and long enough to wrap around all of its four sides.

Pin the felt pieces to the foam to check your dimensions, then remove the pins and stick the felt down using foam mount upholstery adhesive. Allow to dry, then if desired, oversew the adjoining edges at the top, bottom and side of the cube with a needle and sewing thread to give a neat finish.

tweed-covered screen (page 54)

You will need:

A three-panelled self-assembly wooden screen
An iron
2m (2¼yd) tweed fabric, 140cm (54in) wide
Scissors
2m (2¼yd) tartan fabric, 140cm (54in) wide
Adhesive craft spray
A stapler and staples
A tack hammer
300 rust-effect, dome-headed upholstery studs
A bradawl
A screwdriver

The materials listed for this project are sufficient to cover a three-panelled self-assembly screen, each panel measuring 152cm (61in) high and 40cm (16in) wide.

Iron the tweed fabric and lay one panel of the screen on top of the fabric, so that it is 1.5cm (½in) from the edge. Cut out the fabric around the screen, leaving 1.5cm (½in) all the way around. Repeat for the remaining two panels. Then cut out three pieces of ironed tartan fabric in the same way, this time allowing 2cm (¾in) all the way around each panel. Shake the adhesive craft spray well and, holding the can approximately 25cm (10in) away from one panel, spray a good even coat over the entire surface of the screen. Lay the tweed fabric over the top, ensuring that it is flat and there are no air bubbles beneath the panel and the fabric. Fold the edge of the fabric over the rim of the panel, and staple it in place all the way around. Repeat to cover the remaining two panels in the same way.

Turn the screen panels over and spray the reverse side of each panel in turn with adhesive craft spray. Glue down the tartan fabric as before. This time, fold the edge of the fabric around the rim of each panel, then fold it over again to create a neater edge. Then, using the tack hammer, tack in upholstery studs all the way around each panel, approximately 4cm (1½in) apart.

Assemble the screen following the manufacturer's instructions. Use a bradawl to make guide holes through the fabric to enable you to screw the hinges into place.

fabric-covered metal screen (page 67)

You will need:

Scissors
1.5m (1½yd) gingham fabric, 140cm (56in) wide
A tape measure
Pins
A sewing machine
Matching sewing thread
A metal-framed screen
A needle

This quantity of materials is sufficient to cover a two-panelled metal screen, each panel measuring 170cm (68in) high and 65cm (26in) wide. For a different size screen, adapt the materials accordingly.

Cut the gingham fabric in half lengthways so that you have two 1.5m (5ft) strips. Turn under a 1.5cm (½in) hem around the edges of each strip of fabric, and pin. Using a sewing machine threaded with matching sewing thread, stitch the hem around each strip. Remove the pins.

Lay the screen down flat. Place one piece of fabric over the front of one panel of the screen, turning approximately 7cm (3in) over the top and bottom rods so that the fabric is taut. Pin into place at both top and bottom. Starting at the top, gather the fabric evenly across the width, pinning it as you work. Repeat at the bottom of the screen. Then handstitch a neat running stitch along the top and bottom to secure the gathers. Remove the pins. Repeat to cover the second panel of the screen with fabric in the same way.

muslin bed canopy (page 74)

You will need:

A double bed
A tape measure
A saw
A length of 2.5cm (1in) dowel
A bradawl
4 hooks, 2cm (⅝in) long
Emulsion paint: light yellow
A 2.5cm (1in) household paintbrush
4 screw eyes, 1cm (⅜in) wide
Scissors
9m (9¾yd) cerise muslin, 120cm (48in) wide
9m (9¾yd) cinnamon muslin, 120cm (48in) wide
Pins
Matching sewing thread
A sewing machine or needle
An iron

Make sure the bed is positioned where you would like it to be. Measure the width of the bed and saw two lengths of dowel to this size. To attach the dowel lengths to the ceiling, use a bradawl to screw four hooks to the ceiling; position two hooks above the head of the bed, 7.5cm (3in) from the wall. The width between the two should be 5cm (2in) less than the length of the dowel. Secure the remaining two hooks above the foot of the bed; the width between them should be the same as between the first pair.

Paint the dowel lengths with light yellow emulsion paint. Leave to dry. Then secure a screw eye approximately 2.5cm (1in) from each end of both lengths of dowel. Hang the two dowels from the hooks in the ceiling above the bed.

Cut the muslin into 40cm (16in) widths. You will need three cerise and two cinnamon strips. Pin and then sew a cerise strip to a cinnamon strip along one long edge using a french seam; then sew a second cerise strip along the other long edge of the cinnamon strip. Repeat to sew all the strips together, alternating the colours to make a striped length of muslin. Hem around the edges either by hand or by machine. Iron the muslin and drape it over the two dowels to complete the canopy.

page 50   page 10   page 16   page 70

appliqué wall-hanging (page 54)

You will need:

9 pieces of assorted cotton, 25 x 20cm (10 x 8in)
Pins and a needle
A sewing machine and scissors
Matching sewing thread
An iron
9 pieces of assorted tweed and tartan fabric, 19 x 14cm (7½ x 5½in)
1m (1⅛yd) fusible web

Assorted wool and a wool needle
Photocopies of country images
Image transfer solution
1.5m (5ft) cotton duck canvas, 250g (9oz) weight
Paper towels and a sponge
Fabric glue
Assorted felt pens

16 buttons
Brown fabric tape, 2.5cm (1in) wide
A junior hacksaw
45cm (18in) of dowel, 5mm (¼in) thick
Woodstain
A 5cm (2in) household paintbrush
2 small nails and a hammer

Pin the nine pieces of assorted cotton to each other to make a three-row square, with three patches in each row. Stitch all the patches together, taking a 1.5cm (½in) seam. Turn the stitched fabric over and iron the seams flat.

Cut nine pieces of fusible web to the same size as the tweed and tartan rectangles. Lay the patchwork panel down, right side facing. Then lay a tweed or tartan rectangle on top of a patch, sandwiching a fusible web rectangle in between, and iron in place. The fusible web will bond the two layers of fabric to each other. Repeat for each patch of the panel. Using coloured wool, sew large blanket stitches around each tweed rectangle.

Transferring images

Transfer nine photocopied images on to canvas using image transfer solution (page 108). Cut out each transferred image neatly. Using fabric glue, stick one image on to each tweed rectangle. Colour in with felt pens. Sew a button at each corner of the base patches.

Lay the wall-hanging right side down on canvas and cut the canvas to size. Pin the fabrics together. Taking a 1.5cm (½in) seam, sew around three edges, leaving the top unstitched. Turn the right way out through the unstitched edge; iron it flat.

Cut brown fabric tape to match the width of the hanging. Fold it over the top open edges of the hanging to make a sleeve. Pin, then stitch in place. Using a junior hacksaw, cut a length of dowel 8cm (3¼in) longer than the width of the wall-hanging. Coat with woodstain and leave to dry. Insert the dowel through the tape sleeve, and hang the wall-hanging from two small nails hammered into the wall at each side of the dowel.

cotton bunting (page 14)

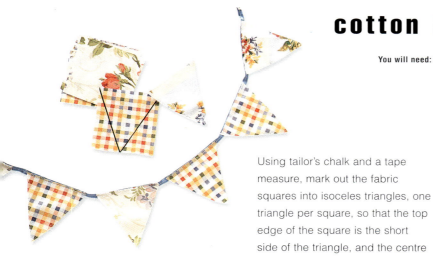

You will need:

Tailor's chalk
A tape measure
Cotton fabric cut into 10cm (4in) squares
Scissors

A sewing machine
Matching sewing thread
Pins
A length of ribbon, 5mm (¼in) wide

Using tailor's chalk and a tape measure, mark out the fabric squares into isoceles triangles, one triangle per square, so that the top edge of the square is the short side of the triangle, and the centre of the bottom edge is the bottom point of the triangle. Cut out the triangles, discarding the remnants of fabric. Then, using a sewing machine, zigzag stitch around all three edges of each triangle.

Pin the short side of each triangle on to the ribbon, leaving approximately 5cm (2in) between each one. Then, using running stitch, sew each triangle on to the ribbon to complete the bunting.

130   THE PROJECTS

chinese banner (page 21)

You will need:

An iron
Black silk, 55 x 150cm (22 x 58in)
2 pieces black silk, 15 x 165cm (6 x 66in)
Black silk, 15 x 85cm (6 x 34in)
Highly decorated red silk, 34 x 150cm (14 x 58in)
Pins and a needle
A sewing machine
Matching sewing thread
Scissors
A protractor
Tailor's chalk
Black cotton or silk for backing, 165 x 85cm (66 x 34in)
Panel pins and a hammer

Iron all the pieces of fabric. Lay the large piece of black silk right side up on a surface, with the short sides horizontal. Place the piece of red silk in the centre of the black silk. Turn the edges under by 1.5cm (½in), pin, then stitch around all sides with matching sewing thread.

Take the two long pieces of black silk and, using a protractor, mark a 45° angle at the bottom of each one, sloping in opposite directions; repeat at each end of the short piece of black silk. When the three pieces of fabric are placed together, they should make three sides of a frame. Sew these 'frame' pieces together along the corner angles. Press the seams, and trim.

Pin the 'frame' pieces to the edges of the large black piece, right sides facing and raw edges matching. Taking a 1.5cm (½in) hem, sew around the two long sides and the bottom edge. Open out again and press all the seams flat. Lay the banner right side down on a piece of black cotton or silk. Stitch around three edges, taking a 1.5cm (½in) seam, leaving one short edge unstitched. Turn the banner the right side out and slipstitch the open edge closed. To hang the banner, tack it on to the picture rail with panel pins.

sari bed throw (page 74)

You will need:

An iron
Indian cotton, 140cm (56in) wide
Scissors
A sari
A tape measure
115g (4oz) wadding
Red lining fabric
Pins
A needle or a sewing machine
Matching sewing thread

Iron the Indian cotton and cut out a 2.5m (3yd) length. Lay the cotton right side down on the floor. Iron the sari and cut a 2m (2¼yd) length; lay this on top of the cotton, right side facing. The sari will be narrower than the cotton leaving a 12cm (5in) border all the way around. Measure a piece of wadding and red lining to the size of the sari. Remove the sari and place the wadding on top of the cotton, leaving the same 12cm (5in) border, then lay the red lining on top; as the sari is fairly transparent, the red lining prevents the wadding showing through. Lay the sari on top of the lining. Fold the cotton up to the sari, enclosing the wadding and lining. Turn under the edges by 2.5cm (1in) and pin to the sari to secure. The neatest way to sew the cotton to the sari is by hand. Mitre the corners for a neat finish.

SOFT FURNISHING PROJECTS

page 10   page 56

construction projects

Wavy-edged shelves (page 62) provide quirky storage space and make a stylish feature in a colourful and cheerful Mexican kitchen.

132 THE PROJECTS

pine plate shelf (page 13)

You will need:

- A tape measure
- A pencil
- A straight edge
- A spirit level
- 8 wooden brackets
- A drill
- Wall plugs
- Screws, 4cm (1½in) and 4.5cm (1¾in) long
- A screwdriver
- Woodfiller
- Medium-grade sandpaper
- Lengths of 12 x 2.5cm (5 x 1in) pine shelving
- A saw
- Lengths of 5 x 1.5cm (2 x ½in) batten
- Wood glue
- Panel pins and a hammer
- Acrylic wood primer
- A 5cm (2in) household paintbrush
- Emulsion paint: pale blue
- Satin acrylic varnish

Measure 1m (1¼yd) from the floor up the wall. Using a straight edge and spirit level, draw a line along the wall to mark this position.

Attaching the brackets

Mark the points where the brackets will be fixed. Each bracket should be placed 1m (1¼yd) apart for stability. Drill holes in the wall at the marked positions and insert a wall plug in each. Attach the brackets to the wall with screws. Fill the screw holes with woodfiller and rub down with sandpaper.

Attaching the shelving

Saw lengths of pine shelving to fit the wall. Cut lengths of batten to match. Attach the batten to the lead edge of the shelving with wood glue; the batten should protrude 2.5cm (1in) above the shelf. Secure with panel pins.

Place the shelving on the brackets and secure in place by screwing two screws through the shelving to each bracket beneath. Fill the screw holes with woodfiller and rub down with sandpaper.

Prime the plate shelf with acrylic wood primer and then paint it with two coats of pale blue emulsion. Seal with two coats of varnish.

wavy shelves (page 62)

You will need:

- A tape measure
- A saw
- 1.5m (5ft) square of MDF, 18mm (¾in) thick
- Medium-grade sandpaper
- A jigsaw
- A length of batten, 5 x 2.5cm (2 x 1in)
- A drill
- Screws, 2.5cm (1in) long
- A screwdriver
- 1m (1¼yd) square of flexible skin ply
- Wood glue
- Panel pins
- A hammer
- A craft knife

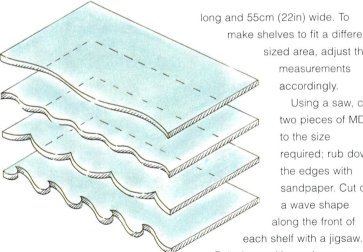

Measure the width of the space to be shelved and work out the size of your shelves; these two shelves were each 95cm (38in) long and 55cm (22in) wide. To make shelves to fit a different-sized area, adjust the measurements accordingly.

Using a saw, cut two pieces of MDF to the size required; rub down the edges with sandpaper. Cut out a wave shape along the front of each shelf with a jigsaw. Rub down with sandpaper.

Saw three lengths of batten for each shelf, one measuring 95cm (38in) and two measuring 47cm (19in) long. Secure the long batten to the back wall, and the shorter battens to the units at each side of the shelf area using screws. Secure the shelves to the battens by inserting screws from above the shelf on to the battens.

Cut a length of skin ply slightly longer than the wavy edge of each shelf, and about 7cm (3in) wide. Secure the skin ply to the edge of each shelf using wood glue and panel pins. Trim the edges with a craft knife, if necessary.

Decorate the shelves to match the wall finish (page 94).

page 16   page 56   page 44   page 24

customized cube unit (page 20)

You will need:

A cube unit, 195cm (78in) tall and 120cm (48in) wide
Tracing paper and a pencil
Two 2.4 x 1.2m (8 x 4ft) sheets of MDF, 18mm (¾in) wide
A protective face mask
A workmate and a jigsaw
A compass and a tape measure
45cm (18in) square of MDF, 6mm (¼in) thick
A drill and a fretsaw
Wood glue and woodfiller
Medium-grade sandpaper
113cm (45in) batten, 5 x 5cm (2 x 2in)
Screws, 5cm (2in) long
A screwdriver
Grey water-based undercoat
A 5cm (2in) household paintbrush
Black acrylic eggshell paint
6 brass plate discs, 20cm (8in) in diameter
Epoxy resin glue
A strong craft knife
16 brass hinges and screws

Enlarge the template on page 155, and transfer it on to thick MDF. Wearing a protective face mask, clamp the MDF in a workmate and cut out the shape with a jigsaw. Draw a circle 23cm (9in) in diameter in the centre of the unit top. Drill a large pilot hole for the entry place, then cut out the circle with a jigsaw. Transfer the circular template (page 154) on to the thin piece of MDF and cut out the shape with a fretsaw. Insert the shape into the cut-out circle and secure with wood glue and filler. When dry, sand the rough edges.

Secure the batten to the top of the unit, set back 18mm (¾in) from the front, with screws. Screw the cut-out unit top to the batten from the front. Fill any holes with woodfiller and sand down when dry. Paint the unit with a grey undercoat, then apply up to three coats of acrylic eggshell paint.

From the thicker MDF, cut four pieces 37cm (15in) square, and four pieces 19 x 37cm (7½ x 15in). Paint all the pieces with grey undercoat, then three coats of black acrylic eggshell; allow to dry.

Stick four of the brass discs to the square doors with epoxy resin glue. Allow to dry for two hours. Cut the other two discs in half with a strong craft knife and glue them to the remaining doors. Attach the doors to the unit, using two hinges for each.

alcove shelves (page 62)

You will need:

Lining paper
A pencil
Scissors
Tracing paper
1m (1⅛yd) square of MDF, 6mm (¼in) thick
A jigsaw
Medium-grade sandpaper
1m (1⅛yd) square of MDF, 12mm (½in) thick
A tape measure
A straight edge
Wood glue
A spirit level
A hammer
Nails, 2.5cm (1in) long
Decorative pillars (available from DIY stores)
Fine surface filler
White acrylic wood primer
A 5cm (2in) household paintbrush
Aqua chalky-finish paint
A drill
Masonry screws, 3.5cm (1⅜in) long
A screwdriver

Make a template for the alcove with lining paper and cut to shape. Transfer this on to the thin MDF and cut out with the jigsaw. Sand down any rough edges.

Decide how many shelves you require and mark these on the thick MDF; they should be 6cm (2⅜in) deep and follow the width of the alcove. Cut the shelves to size using the jigsaw. Mark out on to the backpiece (the thin MDF) where the shelves go and draw in the lines with a straight edge. Fix the shelves into place using wood glue, checking they are level with a spirit level; allow to dry for four hours. Turn the unit over and hammer in some nails to the reverse of each shelf for extra strength. Work out the positions of the pillars and secure these into place top and bottom with nails through the shelves. Fill any gaps with fine filler and rub down with sandpaper when dry.

Paint a coat of white acrylic wood primer over the alcove shelf unit, then paint with an aqua Mexican wall finish (page 94). When dry, attach the unit to the wall with masonry screws. Fill any holes with filler and touch up with the aqua paint.

ebonized overmantel (page 46)

You will need:

A pencil

A tape measure

A straight edge

Two 2.4 x 1.2m (8 x 4ft) sheets of MDF, 18mm (¾in) thick

A workmate

A jigsaw

A protective face mask

A drill

Wood glue

A screwdriver

48 screws, 4.5cm (1¾in) long

A router

Woodfiller

Medium-grade sandpaper

Acrylic wood primer

Household paintbrushes, 2.5cm (1in) and 5cm (2in)

Acrylic blackboard paint

Acrylic varnishing wax

A mutton cloth

This overmantel measures 124cm (50in) wide. If your fireplace is smaller or larger, adjust the size of the overmantel accordingly.

Back and sides

Mark out the dimensions of the back of the mantel on MDF; 113cm (45in) high and 124cm (50in) wide. Using a workmate, and wearing a protective face mask, cut out the back of the mantel with a jigsaw. Mark and cut out four pieces of MDF for the side sections, each 15 x 113cm (6 x 45in). Drill pilot holes at four points down one long side of two of the sections. Insert wood glue into each hole. Then hold up one side section at a time against the back of the overmantel and attach with screws through the back to secure. Repeat to attach the other outer side section.

Then turn the mantel over and mark a line 20cm (8in) in from each side. Drill four holes down each line. Turn the mantel the right way round, hold the inner side sections up to the holes and screw into place from the back.

Top and bottom

Cut out two lengths of MDF 18 x 125cm (7 x 52in). Cut a long curved shape from the centre of one long edge. Using a router, cut a groove along the edge of the pieces. Attach the top of the mantel to the mantel back with four screws, then attach to the outer and inner side sections with four screws. Repeat to attach the bottom.

Mantel shelves

Cut out four pieces of MDF, each 15 x 20cm (6 x 8in). Attach two shelves between each outer and inner side section with screws. Fill any holes with woodfiller and sand down.

Ebonizing

Prime the wood with acrylic wood primer. When dry, apply two to three coats of blackboard paint, allowing two hours between each coat. Lastly apply two coats of varnishing wax. Buff with a mutton cloth to bring up a high shine.

wooden tabletop (page 26)

You will need:

Four 120 x 20cm (48 x 8in) planks of planed wood, 5cm (2in) thick

Three 80 x 10cm (32 x 4in) lengths of planed wood, 2.5cm (1in) thick

A tape measure

Screws, 4cm (1½in) long

A screwdriver

A pencil

A mutton cloth

Water-based antique pine woodstain

Liming wax

2 wrought-iron trestles, 81cm (32½in) wide

Lay the planks of wood on the floor, butting them up together lengthways and ensuring they are level at the top and the bottom. Lay two of the cross struts over the planks, 15cm (6in) from each end. Secure them to the planks with screws. Mark a centre line across the planks and attach the final strut in the same way.

Turn the tabletop over. Using a mutton cloth, wipe a coat of antique pine woodstain over the wood in the direction of the grain. Allow to dry for an hour. Then apply a coat of liming wax, again in the direction of the grain. Lay the wooden tabletop on the wrought-iron trestles to complete the table.

CONSTRUCTION PROJECTS

page 78   page 30   page 16   page 36

revamped dressing table (page 81)

You will need:

A dressing table
A screwdriver
4 Queen Anne legs and appropriate screws
Lining paper
A pencil
Tracing paper
1.5m ((5ft) square of MDF, 18mm (¾in) thick
A jigsaw
A router
Medium- and fine-grade sandpaper
Wood glue
Panel pins
A hammer
A cloth
White acrylic primer
A 5cm (2in) household paintbrush
Emulsion paint: lilac, grey
A small fitch brush
Clear wax
Acrylic satin varnish
A varnish brush
4 knobs

Unscrew the existing dressing table legs and attach new Queen Anne legs in their place. Remove the old drawer knobs and unscrew the old dressing tabletop. Make a template for a new tabletop on lining paper. Transfer this on to MDF and cut out with a jigsaw. Rout the edges and sand down. Apply wood glue to the underside of the tabletop, then secure to the dressing table with panel pins.

Creating an aged paint effect

Sand down the surface. Paint on a coat of white acrylic primer. When dry, apply two coats of lilac emulsion, allowing each coat to dry for two to three hours.

Using a small fitch brush, paint wax on areas that would receive wear and tear. Then apply two coats of grey emulsion over the surface. Using fine sandpaper, lightly rub back those places that were waxed to reveal patches of the base coat. Apply two coats of varnish over the surface, allowing two to three hours' drying time between each coat. Finally, attach the new drawer knobs with screws.

small hexagonal table (page 35)

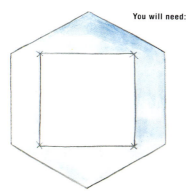

You will need:

A saw
A decorative curtain pole
A tape measure
A hexagonal MDF tabletop
A pencil and a ruler
A drill
4 screws
A screwdriver
Woodfiller
Medium-grade sandpaper
Lengths of fretsawed edging
A mitre block
Wood glue
Panel pins
A hammer
Acylic wood primer
5cm (2in) household paintbrushes
Emulsion paint: ultramarine
Satin acrylic varnish
Copper nails

Saw a curtain pole into four pieces, each 30cm (12in) long. Draw a square on the tabletop, positioned 2.5cm (1in) from the edge. Drill a hole through each corner from the top of the table. Turn the tabletop over. Hold the first piece of curtain pole up to one hole, then insert a screw from the right side of the tabletop to secure. Repeat to attach the remaining pieces of curtain pole to make four legs. Fill the holes with woodfiller; leave to dry, then sand flat.

Measure the hexagonal sides of the table and saw lengths of fretsawed edging 2.5cm (1in) shorter than each side. Mitre the ends of these lengths. Turn the table on its back and glue the edging on to the edge of the underside of the table, positioning it 1.5cm (½in) away from each edge. Secure with panel pins.

Prime the table with acrylic wood primer, then, when dry, apply two coats of ultramarine emulsion. Seal with two coats of acrylic varnish. Finally, hammer in copper nails along the sides of the table, spacing them approximately 7.5cm (3in) apart.

136 THE PROJECTS

bamboo table (page 21)

You will need:

A tape measure
A saw
Nine 3m (3¼yd) lengths of solid bamboo, 2.5cm (1in) wide
A flat-pack table
A pencil
A drill
Screws, 7cm (3in) and 5cm (2in) long
A screwdriver
Pink water-based wood primer
A 5cm (2in) household paintbrush
Red water-based gloss paint
Antique pine tinted wood varnish
A varnish brush
A fine artist's brush
Enamel paint: black, gold

This finished table measures 108cm (43in) long, 77cm (31in) wide and 45cm (18in) high. If your flat-pack table is a different size, alter the dimensions of the bamboo struts accordingly.

Measure and saw 18 lengths of bamboo 108cm (43in) long for the bamboo shelf, and two pieces 67cm (27in) long for the side struts (this measurement allows for the width of the table legs, which are 5cm (2in) thick).

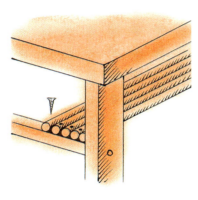

Assemble the flat-pack table following the manufacturer's instructions. Mark a line around each table leg 28cm (11in) from the tabletop. Mark a point in the centre of this line on the outside edge of each leg; this point should be opposite the nearest table leg. Drill a pilot hole in each leg. With someone else's help, hold one of the small bamboo struts between two of the table legs at one end of the table, positioning it at the pilot holes. Using a screwdriver, attach a screw through each table leg and into the bamboo strut to secure the strut in place. Repeat to attach a strut at the other end of the table.

Lay the bamboo lengths over the struts. Using smaller screws, attach the lengths on to the top of the struts, fixing the screws from the top of each length through to the strut beneath.

Apply a lacquer finish over the table (page 103). When dry, apply a coat of tinted wood varnish, working in vertical strokes in one direction only. Allow to dry for three to four hours.

Finally, using a fine artist's brush, paint a thin black line around the outer edge of the tabletop, then paint a thin gold line around the inner edge. Allow to dry for at least three hours.

table on castors (page 43)

You will need:

An industrial metal palette on castors (available from industrial suppliers or dealers in second-hand commercial equipment)
A cloth
Green hammered metal-effect paint
A 2.5cm (1in) household paintbrush
A tape measure
A piece of reinforced wired glass, cut to size
Double-sided sticky pads
4 blocks of wood, 6 x 6cm (2½ x 2½in)
A screwdriver
4 mirror screws and caps
4 rubber washers

Wipe the palette down with a cloth, making sure that it is rust-free, and paint it with a coat of hammered metal-effect paint; allow to dry.

Measure the top of the palette and ask a glazier to cut a piece of reinforced wired glass to fit it exactly; this palette measured 70cm (28in) square. Ask for the sharp edges to be ground down, and for a hole to be drilled at each corner. Using double-sided sticky pads, stick a wooden block to each corner of the painted palette and fix down the glass top by inserting a mirror screw through each hole, through a rubber washer and into the wood. Top with the domed cap of the mirror screw.

CONSTRUCTION PROJECTS **137**

page 70   page 36

indian-style bed posts (page 74)

You will need:
- A wooden bed
- A saw
- 5m (5½yd) of 10 x 10cm (4 x 4in) softwood
- A tape measure
- A small hacksaw
- A drill with a 1.5cm (½in) spade drill bit
- Screws, 10cm (4in) long
- A screwdriver
- Coarse- and fine-grade sandpaper
- A cloth
- Indian rosewood tinted varnish
- A varnish brush

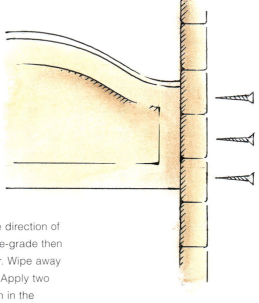

Dismantle the bed but be careful to retain all the fixings in a safe place as you will need these to reassemble it.

Remove any existing bed posts with a saw. For an Indian bed, the posts at the head of the bed are shorter than those at the base. Saw the softwood into two 1.5m (5ft) lengths and two 90cm (3ft) lengths. At intervals around these lengths, saw triangular indentations with a hacksaw to emulate the carving on traditional Indian bed posts.

To attach the posts to the head and base of the bed, drill and countersink two pilot holes in each post, then insert screws through the posts to the head and base respectively to secure. The head and base will then need to be attached to the side struts of the bed in the same way as they were before.

Using the spade bit, drill a hole in the same place on the new posts as on the old ones to enable you to attach the side struts. Before assembling, sand the head and base down in the direction of the grain using coarse-grade then fine-grade sandpaper. Wipe away the dust with a cloth. Apply two coats of tinted varnish in the direction of the grain, allowing the first coat to dry for three to four hours before applying the second. When dry, assemble the bed frame, fitting the cylindrical nuts (part of the bed fixings) into the holes in the new bed posts.

scaffolding bedhead (page 39)

You will need:
- Galvanized scaffolding, tube size D
- 2 elbow clamps
- 2 long tees
- 2 base flanges
- An Allen key

Order scaffolding lengths pre-cut to correspond with the width of your bed. This 135cm (54in) wide bedhead was made out of a single length. Your scaffolding supplier will also be able to provide you with the other materials.

Lay out all the pieces in position on the floor, with the longer lengths lying horizontally at the top, the elbow clamps at the top two corners, the long tees where the second horizontal length meets the vertical, and the base flanges as support at the bottom; refer to the diagram for guidance. With the help of another pair of hands, fit the pieces of scaffolding together using an Allen key. The bedhead is free-standing; position it between the bed and the wall.

To plan more ambitious projects, such as a scaffolding bed, ask for a catalogue from your supplier.

This industrial-looking scaffolding bedhead (page 39) is typical of the minimalist furnishings used in the New York loft.

page 84   page 16   page 56   page 30

decorating sink unit doors (page 89)

You will need:

Double-fronted unit doors
A screwdriver
A pencil
A ruler
A glass brick for each door
A clamp
A workmate
A drill
A jigsaw
A saw
A length of 5 x 2.5cm (2 x 1in) batten, 1m (1¹⁄₉yd) long
Nails
A hammer
Glass brick mortar
A palette knife
A cloth
White acrylic wood primer
A 5cm (2in) household paintbrush
Emulsion paint: ultramarine
Silver acrylic paint
A 1.5cm (½in) flat paintbrush
Satin acrylic varnish

Remove the doors and hinges with a screwdriver; keep the hinges in a safe place. Draw a 20.5cm (8¼in) square on each door where you want to insert the bricks. The bricks are 20cm (8in) square but as they are raised at the front and back edges you need to allow for a slightly larger hole. Clamp each door at a time in a workmate and drill a pilot hole at each corner of the square; then cut out with a jigsaw. Insert the glass brick into the hole; it will protrude about 2cm (¾in) out of each side of the door. Saw two pieces of batten, each 30cm (12in) long; nail them to the back of the door, one on each side of the brick, to hold it securely. Repeat with the second door.

Mix up the glass brick mortar, and apply it around the front of the bricks with a palette knife. Clean off any excess with a cloth. Allow to dry overnight. Paint the unit doors with a coat of acrylic wood primer. When dry, apply two coats of ultramarine emulsion, allowing each coat to dry for two to three hours before applying the next. Paint a thin line of silver paint over the mortar using a flat brush. Finally, seal the doors with two coats of satin acrylic varnish, allowing the first coat to dry before applying the second. When dry, re-attach the hinges and re-hang the doors on the sink unit.

alcove screens (page 20)

You will need:

4 door frames, 40 x 218cm (16 x 87in)
Four 15cm (6in) pieces of batten, 2.5 x 2.5cm (1 x 1in)
Screws, 2.5cm (1in) and screwdriver
Two 85cm (34in) pieces of skirting, 15cm (6in) high
Four 218cm (87in) pieces of batten, 5 x 2.5cm (2 x 1in)
Masonry screws and a drill
Black eggshell paint
A 5cm (2in) household paintbrush
4 pieces of silk, 47 x 223cm (19 x 89in)
Pins and a tape measure
A sewing machine and thread
A stapler and staples
8 hinges and screws
4 small brass knobs

These screens are for two matching alcoves, each 85cm (34in) wide. To make screens for wider or narrower alcoves, adjust the measurements accordingly.

It is advisable to have the door frames made up from mouldings at a framer's. The finished size of each door is 42 x 218cm (16 x 87in) and you will need four doors, two for each alcove.

For each alcove, secure a short batten to each side of the existing skirting inside each alcove using screws; they should be recessed to allow for the new skirting to be aligned with the existing skirting. Attach one piece of 85cm (34in) skirting to the front of each alcove, securing them to the battens with screws from the front. Attach two long battens to the walls at each side of the alcove using masonry screws; position these above the new skirting and flush with the front.

Paint the battens and each frame with two coats of black eggshell paint. Leave to dry.

Turn under the edges of each piece of silk so that each measures 45 x 220cm (18 x 88in). Iron, pin and sew all the way round. Staple a piece of silk into the back of each door frame at top and bottom. Attach the doors to the battens with two hinges for each door. Then secure a brass knob to the centre front of each door.

140 THE PROJECTS

wooden shutters (page 61)

You will need:

16 x 180cm (72in) lengths of planed wood, 10 x 1.5cm (4 x ½in)
A tape measure and a pencil
A saw and tin snips
Coarse-grade sandpaper
A chisel and a plane
A blow torch
A screwdriver and a hammer
Screws, 2.5cm (1in) long
1m x 50cm (40 x 20in) 9-gauge zinc
Large flat-ended roofing clouts
Emulsion paint: red
A 5cm (2in) household paintbrush

This project will make two shutter doors, each with six panels; each shutter is 180cm (72in) high.

Set aside 12 lengths of wood. Measure and mark each of the remaining lengths of wood into three sections, each 60cm (24in) long. Cut the sections with a saw, making the edges a quirky shape. Sand down the rough edges. Roughen up the wood using a chisel and plane, then sand again. Holding a blow torch 25cm (10in) from the surface, scorch some areas of the wood, being careful not to set the wood alight. Sand off any excess scorching.

Lay six lengths of wood flat, ensuring they are level at top and bottom. Measure 15cm (6in) down from the top and lay one of the cross pieces across the lengths. Screw this in place. Repeat again 15cm (6in) from the bottom of the shutters. Screw the final cross piece over the centre of the door. Repeat on the other side of the shutter, then repeat to make a second one.

Using tin snips, cut the zinc into six quirky shapes 60cm (24in) long and hammer these on to the cross bars on one side only of each shutter using roofing clouts.

Woodwash the shutter doors using dilute red emulsion (page 95). Allow to dry, then hang the shutters using strong hinges suitable for doors.

trellis pelmet (page 35)

You will need:

Tracing paper
A pencil
Scissors
1m x 45cm (1⅛yd x 18in) MDF, 12mm thick
A workmate
A protective face mask
A jigsaw
Medium-grade sandpaper
Metal nippers
Roofing clouts
A hammer
Acrylic wood primer
A 5cm (2in) household paintbrush
Emulsion paint: ultramarine
Chocolate brown acrylic colour
Copper gilt cream
A cloth
Nails, 2.5cm (1in) long

Enlarge the pelmet template (page 154) to the dimensions required to fit on to the top of cupboard doors. Trace the enlarged image on to tracing paper, then cut out the shape. Place the tracing paper shape on a sheet of MDF and draw round it with a pencil to make a strong line. Clamp the MDF on to a workmate to secure. Wearing a protective face mask, cut around the shape with a jigsaw. Then rub sandpaper around the edges for a smooth finish.

Decorating the pelmet

Using metal nippers, cut the roofing clouts down to 1.5cm (½in) long, then hammer them into the pelmet at 5cm (2in) intervals all around the edge. Paint the pelmet with acrylic wood primer. When dry, apply two coats of ultramarine emulsion and allow to dry for a further two hours. Dip just the tip of a paintbrush into chocolate brown acrylic colour and brush this over the surface of the pelmet in random brushstrokes, allowing much of the base coat to show through. Leave to dry.

Dip a finger into copper gilt cream and apply a little to each roofing clout. Leave for 15 minutes to set, then buff up with a cloth. Attach the finished pelmet to the top of the trellis-effect doors (page 147) by hammering in a nail at each corner and one at the top.

page 70   page 70   page 36   page 16

kashmiri curtain stays (page 72)

You will need:
- 2 decorative finials
- Burnt umber artist's acrylic colour
- A 2.5cm (1in) household paintbrush
- Tracing paper
- A pencil
- A piece of MDF, 9mm (⅜in) thick
- A workmate
- A protective face mask
- A jigsaw
- Two 20cm (8in) lengths of dowel, 2.5cm (1in) thick
- A drill
- Screws, 3cm (1¼in) long
- A screwdriver
- Gold spray paint

Curtain finials are supplied with a fitting for them to be attached to a pole; keep the fittings to one side. Dry-brush the finials with some burnt umber artist's acrylic colour to age them. Dry overnight. On tracing paper, draw a Kashmiri shape for the backplate, referring to the photograph. Transfer this on to a piece of MDF. Clamp the MDF in a workmate and, wearing a protective face mask, cut out the shape with a jigsaw. Repeat to cut out a second shape.

Attach one length of dowel to the centre of each backplate by inserting screws through the backplate into the dowel; pre-drill the screw holes first. Spray both backplates and dowels with gold paint. Allow to dry thoroughly.

Attach the finials to the dowels using the fittings supplied. Then attach the backplates to the wall, at each lower side of the window, with a screw at the top and bottom of each backplate.

antiqued pelmet (page 72)

You will need:
- A pencil and tracing paper
- A 1.8 x 1.2m (8 x 4ft) sheet of MDF, 9mm (⅜in) thick
- A workmate
- A protective face mask
- A jigsaw
- Medium-grade sandpaper
- A saw
- Lengths of 5 x 2.5cm (2 x 1in) batten
- A drill
- Screws, 5cm (2in) long
- A screwdriver
- Woodfiller
- White acrylic wood primer
- 5cm (2in) household paintbrushes
- Emulsion paint: terracotta
- Antique pine tinted varnish
- A tack hammer
- Decorative studs
- 2 angled brackets

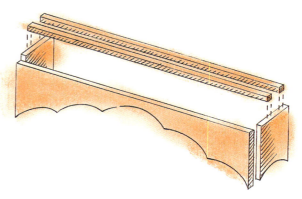

Enlarge the pelmet templates on page 155, and transfer them on to MDF. For this window, measuring 205cm (82in) wide by 162cm (65in) high, the pelmet measured 125cm (98in) long, and 22cm (9in) wide, with a decorative scallop shape along the front and sides. If your window is a different size, adapt these measurements, referring to the diagram.

Clamp the MDF in a workmate and, wearing a protective face mask, cut out the shapes with a jigsaw. Sand any rough edges. Saw two lengths of batten the same length as the front of the pelmet. Drill two pilot holes at the front edge of the side pieces. Secure these side pieces to the front by inserting screws through the front of the pelmet into the side pieces. Fill any holes with woodfiller and sand off when dry.

To make the structure more solid, attach one length of batten along the top of the pelmet, securing it in place to the front of the pelmet with screws; fill as before. Repeat to attach a second batten along the top of the pelmet and secure at the back of the pelmet with screws.

Paint a coat of white acrylic wood primer over the pelmet and allow to dry for one to two hours. Paint on two coats of terracotta emulsion, allowing each coat to dry for two to three hours before applying the next. Dip the tip of a paintbrush into antique pine tinted varnish and dry-brush this over the pelmet using random brushstrokes. Allow to dry for two to three hours. Using a tack hammer, tack decorative studs into the points along the front of the pelmet.

Attach two brackets to the wall with screws (page 133). Place the pelmet over the brackets and screw to the bracket through the front and back batten.

142 THE PROJECTS

canvas screen (page 39)

You will need:

1m (1¼yd) cotton duck canvas, 330cm (132in) wide
A tape measure
Scissors
A stepladder
2 builder's props
4 eyelets
An eyelet punch
A needle and matching thread or fabric glue (optional)
A length of rope

This screen measures 132 x 150cm (53 x 60in). To make a larger or smaller one, adjust the materials as required.

Lay the canvas on the floor, measure the length required and cut out, adding a few centimetres at each side if you want a hem. The width of the cloth will provide the depth of the screen, the variable length, the screen's width. This canvas will be deep enough to make a screen without having to stitch lengths together.

With the help of another pair of hands, and using a stepladder, adjust the builder's props to the height of your room. Fix into position, ensuring that the holes in the top sections face inwards.

Measure 2.5cm (1in) in from each of the fabric's corners and punch the four eyelets into place. Either leave the fabric raw at the edges, or fold a hem over at each of the two drops and tack or glue down to secure.

Using the stepladder, fix the canvas to the props by threading a length of rope through one of the holes at its top, and tie with a knot. Repeat at the bottom of both props but here, where the props have no holes, wrap the rope around the diameter of the prop and knot tightly.

bamboo screen (page 21)

You will need:

A tape measure
A saw
Six 1.5m (5ft) lengths of solid bamboo, 2.5cm (1in) thick
A pencil
A drill
A screwdriver
Screws, 3.5cm (1½in) long
A roll of bamboo screening, 2 x 1.5m (2⅓yd x 5ft)
An industrial staple gun and staples
Black cord
Dome-headed upholstery tacks and a hammer

Measure and saw four lengths of bamboo 1.2m (4ft) long for the outer panel uprights, two lengths 1.5m (5ft) long for the central panel uprights, and six lengths 36cm (15in) long for the horizontal struts.

Measure 15cm (6in) up from the bottom of each of the longer lengths and repeat from the top. Mark with a pencil. Drill a pilot hole at each marked point, then drill a pilot hole into the end of each short strut. Position a small strut at right angles to a 1.5m (5ft) piece of bamboo on the opposite side to the pilot hole. Using a screwdriver, fix a screw through the long piece to the end of the short strut. Repeat to attach a short strut to the top of the bamboo length. Then fix the second 1.5m (5ft) length to the other ends of the short struts to make a frame. Repeat to make two further frames with the 1.2m (4ft) lengths of bamboo.

Lay the frames on the rolled-out bamboo screening and mark out the sizes of the panels required to cover them. Cut out the three panels with a saw. Attach the panels to the reverse side of each frame using an industrial staple gun.

Bind the three frames of the screen together at the top, middle and bottom with black cord. Secure the first knotted end with an upholstery tack on the back of the screen; repeat with the last knot to secure in place.

CONSTRUCTION PROJECTS **143**

page 84

The cool blue glass bricks of this unusual decorative screen (page 86) add a touch of the Mediterranean to the Aegean washroom.

glass brick screen and shelves (page 86)

You will need:

- A tape measure
- A saw
- Lengths of batten, 5 x 2.5cm (2 x 1in)
- Glass bricks
- Screws, 4cm (1½in) long
- Plasterboard wall plugs
- A screwdriver
- Nails, 5cm (2in) long
- A hammer
- Glass brick mortar
- A trowel
- A spirit level
- Glass brick spacers
- A sponge
- White acrylic wood primer
- 5cm (2in) and 10cm (4in) household paintbrushes
- Hardboard
- Panel pins
- Wood glue
- Plaster-covered bandage (available from chemists, surgical suppliers or some craft retailers)
- Textured wall finish mix (page 94)

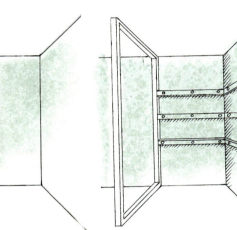

Work out where you want the screen and shelves to be. The screen should be at right angles to one wall and about 65cm (26in) away from and parallel to a second blank wall.

Making the frame

First make up the frame for the screen. Measure the height of the room and saw two lengths of batten to this height. Then stand three glass bricks, short side by short side, allowing 6mm (¼in) space between them, and measure the distance from the first glass brick to the last; cut two lengths of batten to this measurement. Secure one long length of batten on to the wall at the position where you want the screen to be, using screws and plasterboard wall plugs (page 133). Secure one of the short lengths to the floor, coming into the room at right angles to the wall batten, and butting up to it; secure the second short length to the ceiling, parallel to the floor batten. Secure the last length of batten to the battens on the floor and ceiling using nails.

Work out where you want to position the shelves; each shelf will need three lengths of batten to secure it. For each shelf, attach a length of batten from the back of the screen frame to the parallel wall, and one along the parallel wall. Secure into the walls using plasterboard wall plugs and screws (page 133). The third batten can be attached when the glass screen is complete.

Building the glass screen

Mix up the mortar and spread a 6mm (¼in) layer on to the bottom batten of the frame and a little way up each side using a trowel. Spread a layer of mortar along one short side of a glass brick; this will provide the join to the next brick. Place the first brick on the floor batten. Then apply mortar on the next brick and place this next to the first, short side; repeat to complete the first layer. Test that the bricks are level with a spirit level. Insert a spacer at each top corner of the bricks. Repeat this process to build the next layer, and continue upwards to complete the screen. Remove excess mortar with the trowel and allow to dry overnight.

Take the tops of the spacers off by turning them anticlockwise; this will render them invisible. Clean the bricks with a damp sponge. Paint the frame of the screen with two coats of acrylic wood primer, allowing the first coat to dry before applying the second.

Inserting the shelves

For each shelf attach a third batten from the front of the screen to the parallel wall with screws. Next, secure a length of batten to the front of each shelf.

Saw two pieces of hardboard to the size of each shelf; attach one to the top of the three battens, and the other to the underside of the battens, using panel pins and wood glue. Repeat this process for each shelf.

Dip the plaster-covered bandage into water. Lay it all over the shelves and allow to dry for three hours. Apply textured wall finish mix on top to complete.

CONSTRUCTION PROJECTS 145

page 30   page 24   page 30

tented ceiling (page 35)

You will need:

A tape measure
A saw
Lengths of batten, 5 x 2.5cm (2 x 1in)
A pencil and a straight edge
A drill
Wall plugs
A screwdriver
Screws, 4cm (1½in) long
Cotton duck canvas, 3.3m (3½yd) wide, 250g (9oz) weight
Scissors
A stapler and staples
Blue binding tape, 1cm (⅜in) wide
Rust-antiqued, dome-headed upholstery studs
A hammer
A sewing machine
Matching sewing thread
An iron
Emulsion paint: ultramarine
A stencil brush
Walnut brown craft spray

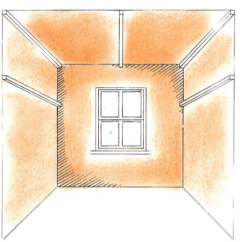

The sloped ceiling in the Moroccan room was ideal for this tent effect; however, a flat ceilinged room can be transformed just as easily.

Measure the length of two opposite walls; these walls should preferably be without doors. Saw five lengths of batten equal to these measurements. Two pieces of batten will be attached to opposite walls at head height, and the three remaining lengths will be attached to the ceiling, one in the centre, and the other two midway between this centre batten and the two side battens, so that all the battens are lying parallel to each other.

Mark the position of the battens on the wall and ceiling using a pencil and straight edge. Then drill holes at 60cm (24in) intervals along the battens. Hold the batten up to the wall or ceiling and mark the position of the holes with a pencil. Pre-drill the holes, and insert a wall plug in each. Using a screwdriver, insert a screw through the batten into each wall plug.

Attaching the canvas

Cut out the amount of canvas you will require. It should be the same length as the room and about 60cm (24in) longer than the width of the room. Then cut the canvas in half lengthways so you can work on one side of the tenting at a time.

Take one of the pieces of canvas, and with someone's help, staple one of the long sides to the lowest batten on one wall. Continue along the batten, folding the canvas under at each end for a neat finish. Using a ladder, lift the canvas up to the next batten, pulling it tight, and staple it into place along the batten as before. Allow the next section of canvas to sag about 10cm (4in) before stapling the ends to the centre batten. Repeat to attach the second piece of canvas.

Attach a length of blue tape over each stapled section of fabric on the ceiling, and secure the tape with upholstery studs.

Making decorative edging

For each lower batten, make a decorative edging to hide the staples. Cut a piece of canvas the length of each batten and 36cm (14in) wide. Fold the canvas lengthways so it is 18cm (7in) wide. Then, using a pencil and tape measure, mark castellations 10cm (4in) square all along the open side of the folded canvas. Using a sewing machine threaded with matching thread, stitch along the marked castellations, leaving an opening at one edge. Cut off the excess fabric and turn the edging the right way out, teasing out the corners. Stitch the opening closed and iron flat. Repeat to make the edging for the opposite wall. Using the single star stencil (see template on page 150), stencil along the castellations on each edging, using ultramarine emulsion (page 95). Allow to dry.

Hold the edging up to the wall, so that the straight edge matches the stapled tent edge. Staple along the batten to attach the edging, then fold down the edging to hide the staples. Tack into place with upholstery studs. Repeat to attach the edging on the opposite wall. To age the tenting, spray patches of brown craft spray along the edges.

146 THE PROJECTS

CD pillar (page 28)

You will need:

A 115 x 18.5cm (46 x 7¼in) sheet of MDF, 6mm (¼in) wide

Three 18.5 x 5cm (7¼ x 2in) semi-circles of MDF, 6mm (¼in) thick

A 115 x 25cm (46 x 10in) sheet of flexible skin ply

Panel pins

A tack hammer

A craft knife

A magnetic catch and screws

A screwdriver

A flat-pack CD tower, 115cm (46in) high

2 hinges and screws

Lay the MDF sheet flat with a short side at the top. Attach two MDF semi-circles to the top and bottom of the MDF with panel pins. Add the third semi-circle in the centre. Lay the skin ply over the top, securing it with panel pins along the long edge of the MDF, over the semi-circles, and along the last long edge; trim off any excess ply with a craft knife. This is the door.

Screw a magnetic strip to the top inside corner of the door and the other part of the magnetic catch to the CD tower. Attach the door to the tower with hinges using the appropriate screws. Decorate as for the wall finish (page 93).

trellis-effect doors (page 32)

You will need:

A wooden cupboard with full-length doors

A screwdriver

A pencil and a straight edge

A workmate and a jigsaw

A protective face mask

A tape measure

1.5m x 60cm (60 x 24in) machine-cut fretwork

Panel pins and a hammer

A saw

6m (6½yd) of batten, 2.5 x 2.5cm (1 x 1in)

Wood glue

Metal nippers

Roofing clouts

Paints and paintbrushes (page 141)

1.5m (60in) cotton fabric

These materials are sufficient to make trellis-effect doors for a cupboard measuring 165cm (66in) high by 37cm (15in) wide.

Remove the doors from the cupboard, retaining the hinges and screws for re-attaching. Lay the doors flat and, using a pencil and straight edge, mark a line around the inside of the doors 5cm (2in) away from the edge. Clamp the doors one at a time in a workmate and, wearing a protective face mask, cut out the inside of the doors with a jigsaw. Measure the resulting gap; this should be the same on each door.

Mark out two panels on the fretwork, each 2.5cm (1in) larger all around than the gaps in the door. Clamp the fretwork in a workmate and cut out these marked panels with a jigsaw. Lay one fretwork panel over each door to cover the gap, and secure in place with panel pins.

Then, saw lengths of batten to fit around the sides of the fretwork panels, overlapping the edges. Secure this frame in place on both doors with wood glue, then tap in panel pins for added security.

Using metal nippers, cut down the roofing clouts until they measure 2.5cm (1in). Hammer these into the frame of each door 30cm (12in) apart on the verticals of the frame, and 15cm (6in) apart on the horizontals.

Re-hang the doors on the cupboard, then paint the doors and cupboard using the same colours and paint technique as for the pelmet (page 141) and leave to dry. As a finishing touch, staple a piece of coloured cotton fabric on to the reverse of each cupboard door; staple it at intervals all around the edge, ensuring it is taut. The fabric will be visible through the gaps in the fretwork.

CONSTRUCTION PROJECTS **147**

page 10   page 16

beach house day bed (page 14)

You will need:

A tape measure
A pencil
2 sheets of 2.4 x 1.2m (8 x 4ft) MDF, 18mm (¾in) thick
A workmate
A protective face mask
A jigsaw
A saw
Lengths of batten, 5 x 5cm (2 x 2in)
Medium-grade sandpaper
A straight edge
A drill with a 2.5cm (1in) spade bit
A screwdriver
Screws, 2.5cm (1in) long
Woodfiller
4 industrial castors
White acrylic wood primer
A 5cm (2in) household paintbrush
Emulsion paint: pale blue
4m (4½yd) cotton fabric
Scissors
Matching sewing thread
A sewing machine
80 x 185cm (32 x 74in) upholstery foam, 10cm (4in) deep

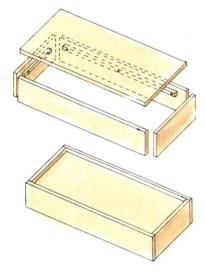

Mark the MDF into the following lengths: two pieces 20 x 80cm (8 x 32in), two pieces 20 x 185cm (8 x 74in), and one piece 80 x 185cm (32 x 74in). Clamp the MDF in a workmate and, wearing a mask, cut out the pieces using a jigsaw.

Next saw the battens into two lengths 50cm (20in) and two lengths 112cm (45in). Sand down.

Take the short battens and short pieces of MDF. Measure 5cm (2in) from one long side of the MDF and draw a line to mark the position. Drill two holes 15cm (6in) from each side of the MDF, along this marked line. Lay one piece of batten on a flat surface and place the piece of drilled MDF on top. Insert a screw into each of the drilled holes to the batten beneath to attach the batten to the MDF. Repeat with the other short piece of MDF and batten.

Repeat this process with the long pieces of MDF and batten, but this time drilling four holes through the MDF and attaching the batten with four screws.

Take one of the long sections and drill two holes at the edge of each short side. Place one of the short pieces of MDF at right angles to the long piece with its edge abutting the drilled holes. Ensure that the battens are nearer the top of the two pieces than the bottom.

Screw through the drilled holes from the outer side of the long piece to attach. Repeat this process to attach the other pieces of MDF. Then join them all together in the same way to form a box with all the battens uppermost.

Next, lay the large piece of MDF in the box so that it rests on the battens. Drill two holes at each side of the box, level with the MDF sheet and insert screws through the holes into the MDF sheet to secure. Fill any screw holes with woodfiller, then sand down.

Once the box is made, screw an industrial castor to each corner of the box. Prime the box with acrylic wood primer, then woodwash the base with dilute pale blue emulsion in the direction of the grain.

Upholstering the day bed

Cut two rectangles of cotton fabric measuring 87 x 192cm (35 x 77in). With right sides together, machine stitch the pieces together around three and a half sides, taking a 1.5cm (½in) seam. Turn the cover the right way out through the gap, then insert the foam block.

Slipstitch the gap closed.

Drill a few holes in the MDF sheet to allow for air flow and prevent rotting. Place the covered foam block in the box.

Making low seating

Follow the above instructions to make low seating (page 35), with the following differences.

The MDF measurements are as follows: two lengths 34 x 125cm (14 x 50in), two lengths 34 x 62.5cm (14 x 25in), and one length 62.5 x 125cm (25 x 50in).

Apply a sandstone paint effect to the finished MDF box. Dip a damp sponge into white emulsion and dab this randomly over the box. Repeat using burnt sienna acrylic colour, but this time only over certain areas of the surface, and blending the paint into the white. While the paint is still wet, skim a lily bristle brush over the surface to soften and blend the colours further. Allow to dry.

Finally, instead of using one block of foam, use two 62.5cm (25in) square foam blocks, 10cm (4in) deep.

chinese day bed (page 20)

You will need:
- 2 sheets of 2.4 x 1.2m (8 x 4ft) MDF 32mm (1¼in) thick
- A pencil
- A straight edge
- A tape measure
- A protective face mask
- A workmate
- A jigsaw
- A compass
- A drill
- A screwdriver
- Screws, 6cm (2½in) long
- Woodfiller
- Medium-grade sandpaper
- Tracing paper
- 45cm (18in) square sheet of MDF, 6mm (¼in) thick
- A fretsaw
- Wood glue
- Grey water-based primer
- A 5cm (2in) household paintbrush
- Black acrylic eggshell paint

On the thick MDF mark out the following pieces using a pencil and straight edge: one piece measuring 70 x 175cm (28 x 70in), two pieces measuring 70 x 65cm (28 x 26in), one piece measuring 30 x 169cm (12 x 67½in), and two pieces measuring 70 x 20cm (28 x 8in). Wearing a protective face mask and with the MDF clamped in a workmate, cut out the pieces with a jigsaw.

On the two pieces measuring 70 x 65cm (28 x 26in), draw a circle 23cm (9in) in diameter, centred and 5cm (2in) from one long side. Make a large pilot hole for the entry place, then cut out the circles with a jigsaw.

Lay the long piece out first and with another pair of hands hold the two 70 x 65cm (28 x 26in) pieces at right angles to each short side of the long piece. The cut-out circles should be near the top of each side piece. Drill two pilot holes at either end and screw the side pieces to the base. Insert the 30 x 169cm (12 x 67½in) piece upright into the back of the day bed, so that it is between the two side pieces and resting on the MDF base. Drill two pilot holes for each side at the back of the side pieces and screw through the side pieces into the back piece to secure. Then turn the unit upside-down and screw through the base into the back to secure further.

With the unit still upturned, mark a line 25cm (10in) from each side. Turn the unit over and position the two pieces measuring 70 x 20cm (28 x 8in) underneath, standing them vertically as legs. Make sure they are aligned. Screw down through the base into the legs from the top. Fill any screw holes with woodfiller and sand down.

Transfer the template (page 154) twice on to the thin piece of MDF and cut the shapes out with a fretsaw. Insert the shapes into the cut-out circles at each side of the day bed and secure with wood glue and filler. Sand down.

Apply an undercoat of grey primer, then paint up to three coats of black acrylic eggshell on top, allowing each coat to dry before applying the next. To upholster the day bed, either make your own cushions using upholstery foam (page 148) or, as here, have seating made by a professional upholsterer.

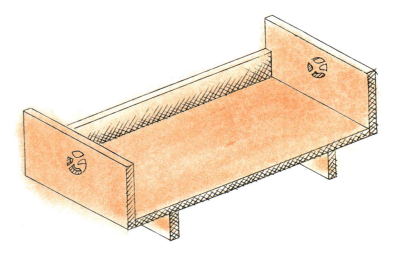

CONSTRUCTION PROJECTS

templates

This section contains the templates for some of the projects which are featured earlier in this book. They are designed to save you time when undertaking any of these projects. To use a template, enlarge it to the required size on a photocopier, ensuring that you keep all the templates from one project in proportion to each other. Then trace around the template and transfer on to card, paper, MDF, or whatever the project calls for.

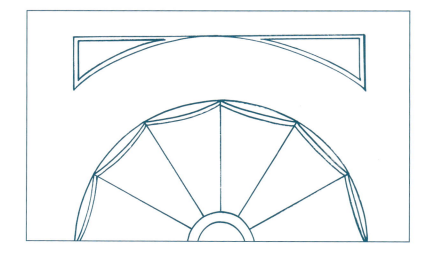

Page 98: *Trompe-l'oeil* arch

template of interlocking cross   template of star

Page 97: Stencilled mosaic-effect wall

Page 103: Decorated kitchen cupboard doors

Page 96: *Trompe-l'oeil* panelling

Page 95: Stencilled surface; page 110: Jewelled cross

Page 96: Stencilled frieze

TEMPLATES **151**

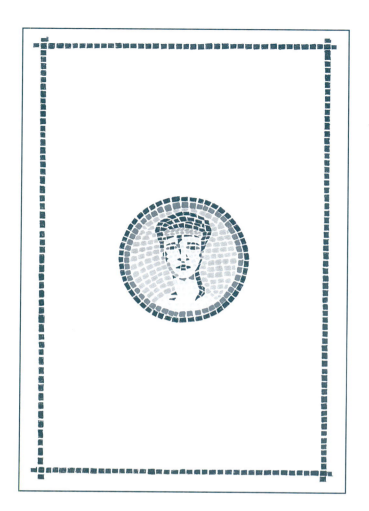

outline of head

Above: Enlarge the outline of the head and transfer it on to the centre of the canvas, as shown in the diagram (far left). Then paint the design referring to the photograph (left) for guidance on colours.

Page 99: Canvas floorcloth

Page 112: Display niche

152 TEMPLATES

Page 106: Punched tin lantern

Page 115: Woven paper bowl

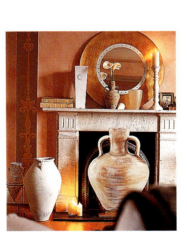

Page 113: Urn firescreen

TEMPLATES **153**

Page 117: Tasselled sari cushions

Page 134: Customized cube unit; page 149: Chinese day bed

Page 141: Trellis pelmet

template of pelmet front

template of pelmet sides

Above and left: These templates are all sections of the pelmet in the Indian bedroom (page 72). They may be enlarged to whatever size you require, but they must be enlarged in proportion to each other for the project to work.

Page 142: Antiqued pelmet

Right: This circular template can be used for drawing out circles on sheet brass for the brass doors in the customized cube unit (left and page 134) if brass discs are unavailable. Transfer the template in the usual way then cut out the circle with tin snips.

Page 103: Découpaged screen; page 134: Customized cube unit

TEMPLATES **155**

stockists and suppliers

The following suppliers will be able to provide you with materials and equipment needed for the projects in this book.
For suppliers marked with ◆ please see acknowledgments on page 160.
✉ indicates that a mail-order service is available.

◆ **AERO** ✉
347-349 Kings Road,
London SW3 5ES
0208 351 0511
Standard office filing cabinets

◆ **AMPHORA**
155 Goldhawk Road,
London W12 8EN
0208 749 2320
Props for Tuscan day room

ANGELIC
194 Kings Road,
London SW3 5XP
0207 351 1557
Suppliers of candles, lanterns and glass nuggets; branches countrywide

ANTA SCOTLAND LTD
Fearn, Tain, Ross-shire,
Scotland 1V20 1XW
01862 832477
Makers of plaids, tartans and related home accessories

THE BEAD SHOP
21a Tower Street,
London WC2H 9NS
0207 240 0931
Suppliers of beads, thread and wire

◆ **BENCHMARK ART FURNITURE** ✉
291 Westbourne Grove,
London W11 2HR
0207 229 4179
Manufacturers of highly decorative upholstery studs

◆ **EMMA BERNHARDT** ✉
301 Portobello Road,
London W10 5TE
0208 960 2929
Stockist of Mexican decorative accessories and homewear

◆ **CELIA BIRTWELL**
71 Westbourne Park Road,
London W2 5QH
0207 221 0877
Designer of handprinted silk and voile fabrics

BIZ
Mill Marsh Lane,
Brimsdown, Enfield
Middlesex EN3 7QA
0208 443 3300
Major suppliers of sheet metal

◆ **BLADERUBBER STAMPS** ✉
2 Neals Yard, London
WC2 9DP
0207 379 7391
Suppliers of rubber stamps, water-based ink pads and stencils

◆ **THE BLUE DOOR**
77 Church Road,
London SW13 0DQ
0208 748 9785
Props for Swedish bedroom

◆ **BRITISH FELT** ✉
14 Drakes Mews,
Crownhill, Milton Keynes,
Buckinghamshire MK8 0ER
01908 263304
Craft felt in many colours

◆ **BROADWICK SILKS**
9-11 Broadwick Street,
London W1V 1FN
0207 734 3320
Suppliers of a wide range of Chinese silks, velvets and fake furs

◆ **F H BRUNDLE**
Riverside House, Bow
Industrial Park, Carpenters
Road, London E15 2DZ
0208 525 7100
Scaffolding

◆ **THE CANE STORE** ✉
207 Blackstock Road,
Highbury Vale, London
N5 2LL
0207 354 4210
Suppliers of raw materials such as chair cane, bamboo, rattan

◆ **CASA PAINT CO**
PO Box 77, Thame,
Oxfordshire OX9 3FZ
01296 770139
Manufacturers of Mediterranean-style paints that dry to a chalky finish

THE COPYRIGHT-FREE BOOKSHOP ✉
18 Earlham Street,
London WC2N 9LN
0207 836 2111
Stockists of Dover Books' copyright-free source books

L. CORNELLISEN AND SON ✉
105 Great Russell Street,
London WC1B 3RY
0207 636 1045
Suppliers of pigment and specialist art supplies

◆ **CROWN PAINTS**
Crown House, Hollins
Road, Darwen, Lancashire
BB3 0BG
01254 704951
Paint in a wide range of colours

DALER ROWNEY LTD
12 Percy Street,
London W1A 2B
0207 636 8241
Manufacturers of a wide range of standard artist's supplies

◆ **DAMASK FURNISHING & FINERY LTD**
Broxholme House,
New Kings Road,
London SW6 4AA
0207 731 3553
Props for Swedish bedroom

◆ **DEBENHAMS**
Oxford Street, London W1
0207 580 3000
Props for Aegean washroom

◆ **DECORATIVE LIVING**
55 New Kings Road,
London SW6 4SE
0207 736 5623
Props for Moorish den and Scottish study

◆ **DESCAMPS LTD**
197 Sloane Street,
London SW1X 9QX
0207 235 6957
Props for Kashmiri bedroom and Parisian boudoir

◆ **DULUX**
ICI Paints, Wexham Road,
Slough, Berkshire SL2 5DS
01753 550555
Paint in thousands of colours

◆ **R DYLON INTERNATIONAL LTD**
Worsley Bridge Road,
Lower Sydenham, London
SE26 5HD
0208 663 4801
Dye manufacturers and suppliers

ELEPHANT LTD
230 Tottenham Court
Road, London W1P 9AE
0207 637 7930
Props for Chinese living room

ELLIS AND FARRIER ✉
20 Beak Street, London
W1R 3HA
0207 629 9964
Suppliers of beads, jewels and studs

THE ENGLISH STAMP COMPANY ✉
Sunnydown, Worth
Matravers, Dorset
BH19 3JP
01929 439117
Manufacturers of rubber stamps and paints with a made-to-order service

◆ **CHRISTOPHER FARR**
212 Westbourne Grove,
London W11 2RH
0207 792 5761
Props for Parisian boudoir

◆ **FIRED EARTH PLC** ✉
Twyford Mill, Oxford Road,
Adderbury, Oxfordshire
OX17 3HP
01295 812088
Manufacturers of historical paints, natural flooring tiles and fabrics

FORMICA LTD
Coast Road, North Shields,
Tyne & Wear NE29 8RE
0191 259 3000
Suppliers of laminates for surfaces, including metallics; samples available

◆ **TIMNEY FOWLER** ✉
388 Kings Road,
London SW3 5UZ
0207 352 2263
Designers of strong monochromatic prints inspired by classical images; props for Tuscan day room

(PHOTOCOPY onto A4)

"The Most Beautiful VILLAGES of FRANCE"
(T&H) 1990.

Dominique Repérant
(Photo. + Writer.)

MINISTRY of CULTURE / Ministère de la Culture.

MH (Monument historique / Historic Monument)

Inv. MH. (Inventaire supplementaire des Monuments historiques / Supplementary Inventory of Hist° Mons)

→ Laws governing their preservation / restoration are less stringent).

FOXELL AND JAMES
57 Farringdon Road,
London EC1M 3JB
0207 405 0152
Suppliers of a wide range of specialist paints and varnishes

◆ **GWB BEDDING**
Unit 10, Hanover Trading Estate, North Road,
London N7 9DH
0207 619 0294
Beds and bedding

◆ **HABITAT (HEAD OFFICE)**
The Heals Building,
196 Tottenham Court Road, London W1 9LD
0207 255 2545
Furniture and accessories; contact for local store

◆ **HAUTE DECO**
556 Kings Road, London
SW6 2DZ
0207 736 7171
Suppliers of resin and metal designer knobs and door furniture

◆ **HEPHER DIY**
120 Beulah Road,
Thornton Heath, Surrey
CR7 8JF
0208 653 7913
Wide range of wood and joinery supplies

◆ **THE HOLDING COMPANY**
241-245 Kings Road,
London SW3 5EL
0207 352 1600
Props for Parisian boudoir and Aegean washroom

HOMECRAFTS DIRECT ✉
PO Box 38, Leicester
LE1 9BU
0116 251 3139
Suppliers of arts and crafts materials, including mosaic equipment

◆ **INDIGO**
275 New Kings Road,
London SW6 4RD
0207 384 3101
Props for Kashmiri bedroom

◆ **JAIPUR DESIGNS**
13 Goodge Street
London W1P 1FE
0207 636 5560
Props for Kashmiri bedroom

◆ **JALI LTD**
Aspley House, Chartham,
Canterbury, Kent CT4 7HT
01227 831710
Suppliers of decorative unpainted edge trims and fretwork panels

◆ **KASBAR WORLD OF INTERIORS**
300 Thornton Road,
Croydon, Surrey
0208 689 1818
Props for Moorish den

◆ **KEY INDUSTRIAL EQUIPMENT LTD** ✉
Blackmore Road, Ebblake Industrial Estate, Verwood, Dorset BH31 6AT
01202 827371
Industrial furniture and accessories

◆ **CATH KIDSTON** ✉
8 Clarendon Cross,
London WII 4AP
0207 221 4000
Wonderful collection of kitsch fabrics and wallpapers, including second hand

◆ **LONDON GRAPHIC CENTRE**
16-18 Shelton Street,
London WC2H 9JJ
0207 240 0095
Lightboxes

◆ **MALABAR COTTON CO**
31-33 The Southbank Business Centre, Ponton Road, London SW8 5BL
0207 501 4200
Suppliers of cotton and silk upholstery and curtain fabrics

◆ **IAN MANKIN** ✉
271 Wandsworth Bridge Road, London SW6 2TX
0207 371 8825
Suppliers of natural fabrics

◆ **MARK MAYNARD ANTIQUES**
651 Fulham Road, London
SW6 5PU
0207 731 3533
Props for Swedish bedroom

◆ **MORPLAN** ✉
PO Box 54, Temple Bank,
Riverway, Harlow, Essex
CM20 2TS
01279 435333
Commercial clothes rails and shopfitting equipment

◆ **MUJI** ✉
39 Shelton Street,
Covent Garden, London
WC2H 9HJ
0207 379 1331
Japanese furniture, clothes and accessories

◆ **RAY MUNN LTD**
861-863 Fulham Road
London SW6 5HP
0207 736 9876
Paints and specialist paint products

◆ **NEAL STREET EAST**
5 Neal Street, London
WC2H 9PU
0207 240 0135
Ethnic decorative accessories and homeware; props for Chinese living room

PAINT LIBRARY
5 Elystan Street, Chelsea Green, London SW3 3NT
0207 823 7755
Specialist paints in historical and contemporary colours, and coloured metallic paints

◆ **GEORGE PEDERSEN INTERIORS LTD**
152 Upper Street, London
N1 1RA
0207 359 5655
Props for Tuscan day room

◆ **PENTONVILLE RUBBER**
104 Pentonville Road,
London N1 9JB
0207 837 4582
All grades of foam cut to size

E PLOTON (SUNDRIES) LTD ✉
273 Archway Road,
London N6 5AA
0208 348 0315
Suppliers of gilding equipment

◆ **RUSSELL AND CHAPPLE LTD** ✉
23 Monmouth Street,
London WC2 9DE
0207 836 7521
Artist's supplies, including cotton duck and canvas

◆ **DAVID SCOTCHER INTERIORS**
285 Upper Street,
London N1
0207 354 4111
Props for Parisian boudoir

SCREWFIX DIRECT ✉
Houndstone Business Park, Yeovil, Somerset
BA22 8RT
0500 414141
Suppliers of screws, fixings and tools

◆ **SCUMBLE GOOSIE** ✉
Lewiston Mill, Toadsmoor Road, Stroud,
Gloucestershire GL5 2TB
01453 731305
Suppliers of unpainted MDF furniture

◆ **SERVICEPOINT**
69-85 Old Street, London
EC1V 9HX
0207 608 2011
A0 size copies mounted on foam board

SOUTHERN CRAFT SUPPLIES
25 Upton Avenue,
Southwick, West Sussex
BN4 4WP
01273 870804
Catalogue company for pewter sheet and other modelling supplies

TRAVIS PERKINS (HEAD OFFICE)
Lodge Way House, Lodge Way, Harlestone Road,
Northamptonshire NN5 7UG
01604 752424
Countrywide retailers of wood and joinery supplies; contact for local store

EDGAR UDNY AND CO LTD
The Mosaic Centre Ltd,
314 Balham High Road,
London SW17 7AA
0208 767 8181
Importers and distributors of mosaics and tiles

◆ **WARRIS VIANNI** ✉
85 Goldbourne Road,
London W10 5NL
0208 964 0069
Exotic silks and organzas from India and Thailand

◆ **VIRGINIA ANTIQUES**
98 Portland Road, London
W11 4LQ
0207 727 9908
Props for Parisian boudoir

◆ **DAVID AND CHARLES WAINWRIGHT**
63 Portobello Road,
London W11 3DB
0207 727 0707
Props for Kashmiri bedroom

◆ **WYCHWOOD DESIGN** ✉
Viscount Court,
Brizenorton, Oxfordshire
OX18 3QQ
01993 851575
Manufacturers of a range of unfinished wooden frame furniture

index

Page numbers in italic refer to the illustrations

A
Aegean washroom, 84-9, *86-9*
aged plaster wall finish, 93
alcove screens, 140
alcove shelves, 134
aluminium tiles, 58-61, *58*, 99
antiqued pelmet, 142
antiquing wax, 20
appliqué wall-hanging, 53, 54, 130
aqua pigment paint, 58
arch, *trompe-l'oeil*, 98
architectural elements, Italian look, 24
artwork, canvas, 110

B
bamboo:
    lamps, 21, *23*, 107
    screen, 143
    table, 137
banner, Chinese, 21, 131
banner curtains, 122-3
bathroom, Aegean washroom, 86-9, *86-9*
bath panel, zinc, 89, *89*, 102
beach house day bed, 148
beach house style, 10-15, *10-15*
bedrooms:
    Kashmiri bedroom, 72-7, *72-7*
    Parisian boudoir, 80-83, *80-83*
    Swedish bedroom, 66-9, *66-9*
beds:
    Indian-style bed-posts, 138
    Kashmiri bedroom, 74, *75*
    muslin bed canopy, 129
    New York loft look, 39, *42*
    scaffolding bedhead, 138

Berber tents, 31
blinds:
    canvas, 14, *14*, 34, 35, 125
    Kashmiri bedroom, *72*
    lace, 89, *89*, 126
    muslin, *20*, 21
    tie blinds, 122
bolster cushions, 67-8, *67*, 119
bookcases, Scottish look, 53-4, *55*
boudoir, Parisian, 78-83, *78-83*
bowls:
    metal fruit bowl, *62*, 115
    woven paper bowl, *62*, 115
bows, picture, *68*, 108
bricks, glass, 86, *86*, 89
Buddhism, 16
bunting, *12*, 14, 130
bunting cushions, 118
butler's trays, 54, *54*

C
cafe curtains, 68, *68*
cafe table, chrome-effect, 112
candle sconces, 76, *76*, 105
candles, 32, *49*
canvas:
    artwork, 110
    blinds, 14, *14*, 34, 35, 125
    painted canvas floorcloth, 28, *29*, 99
    screens, 39, *40-41*, *43*, 143
    tented ceiling, 146
castors, table on, 137
CD towers, 28, *28*, 147
ceilings, tented, *34*, 146
chairs:
    beach house style, *15*
    Georgian parlour, *49*
    Kashmiri bedroom, 76
    Mexican look, *60*
    New York loft look, 39
    re-covered, 126
    Scottish look, *52*, 54, *55*
chaises, Parisian boudoir, *80*, 81

Chinese banner, 131
Chinese day bed, 149
Chinese look, 16-23, *16-23*
chrome-effect cafe table, 112
clothes rails, 39, *42*
coffee table, Chinese look, *18*
coir matting, 72
collection boxes, 54, *54*
colour:
    Aegean washroom, 86
    beach house style, 13
    Chinese look, 20
    Georgian parlour, 46
    Italian look, 26
    Kashmiri bedroom, 72
    Mexican look, 58
    Moroccan look, 31, 32
    Parisian boudoir, 81
    Scottish look, 53
    Swedish bedroom, 67
column pedestals, 26-8, *28*, 114
corbels, *29*
cotton bunting, 130
crosses:
    jewelled cross, 110
    maltese cross, 119
cube unit, customized, 134
cupboards:
    decorated cupboard doors, 103
    fabric inserts in cupboard doors, 102
    Mexican look, *58-9*, 61
    Moroccan look, 32-5, *35*
    Swedish bedroom, *66*, 67
    trellis-effect doors, 147
curtain poles, 28
curtain stays, Kashmiri, 142
curtains:
    banner curtains, *20*, 21, 122-3
    cafe curtains, 68, *68*
    Italian look, 29, *29*
    Kashmiri bedroom, 72-4
    lined curtains, 121
    New York loft look, 42

Parisian boudoir, 81
    sari curtains, 125
    Scottish look, 53-4
    stamped voile curtains, 121
    with tabs, 123
cushions:
    beach house style, *15*
    bolster cushion, 67-8, *67*, 119
    bunting cushions, 118
    Chinese look, 21
    fringed cushion, 120
    Italian look, *28*, *29*
    Kashmiri bedroom, 74, *77*
    Moroccan look, 35
    Parisian boudoir, *80*, 81
    patched silk cushions, 118
    tasselled sari cushions, 117
    with voile pockets, 120

D
dado rails, Scottish look, 53, *54*
day beds:
    beach house, 14, *14*, 148
    Chinese look, 20, 22-3, 149
    Italian look, *28*, 29
day room, Tuscan, 26-9, *26-9*
découpage screen, *19*, 103
den, Moorish, 30-37, *30-37*
display niche, 73, 76, 112
doors:
    decorated cupboard doors, 103
    fabric inserts, 102
    sink unit doors, *88*, 140
    trellis-effect doors, 147
dressing tables, 81, *82*, 136
driftwood, 14

E
ebonized overmantel, 135
engravings, *47*, 48-9, 101

F
fabric-covered metal screen, 129
fabric inserts, cupboard doors, 102
filing cabinets, 39
fireplaces:
    ebonized overmantel, 135
    Georgian parlour, 46, *48*
    Italian look, 28
    Mexican look, *60*
firescreen, urn, *27*, 28, 113
floor cushions, 35
floors:
    Aegean washroom, 89
    beach house style, 13
    Chinese look, 20
    Georgian parlour, 46, *46*
    Kashmiri bedroom, 72
    Mexican look, 61
    Moroccan look, 32
    New York loft look, 39, *41*
    painted canvas floorcloths, 28, *29*, 99
    painted 'rugs', 46, *48*
flowers, Scottish look, *53*
foam lounger, 128
frames:
    pewter-covered mirror frame, 111
    silvered mirror frame, 111
French look, 78-83, *78-83*
frescoes, Italian look, 26
fretwork, 35
friezes, stencilled, *66*, 67, 96
fringed cushion, 120

G
Georgian parlour, 46-9, *46-9*
gingham, 67
    lampshade, 105

glass ball lamp base, 82, *82*, 104
glass brick screen, 86, *86*, 89, 145
glass nuggets, jewelled cross, 110
Greek look, 84-9, *84-9*

H
hat boxes, 68, *69*, 83
headboards, Swedish bedroom, 67
hexagonal table, 136
Hindu temples, 70

I
Indian look, 70-77, *70-77*
Indian-style bed-posts, 138
inked silhouettes, 101
Irish Georgian look, 46-9, *46-9*
iron, Italian look, 26, *26*
Italian look, 24-9, *24-9*

J
jewelled cross, 110

K
Kashmiri bedroom, 70-7, *72-7*
Kashmiri curtain stays, 142
kitchens:
    decorated cupboard doors, 103
    Mexican, 58-63, *58-63*
Knights Templar, 89

L
lace blinds, 89, *89*, 126
lacquer:
    Chinese look, *19*, 21, 92
    découpage screen, 103
lampshades:
    bamboo lamp, 107
    covered lampshade, 106
    gingham lampshade, 105
    parchment

lampshade, 107
Parisian boudoir, 80, 82, *82*
piped lampshades, 104
striped and beaded lampshades, 104
lanterns, *32-4*
punched tin lanterns, *86*, 89, 106
Larsson, Carl, 65, *66*
leather pouffe, stamped, 127
lighting:
bamboo lamp, 107
Chinese look, 21, *23*
covered lampshade, 106
gingham lampshade, 105
glass ball lamp base 82, *82*, 104
Italian look, 29
Moroccan look, *32-4*
parchment lampshade, 107
Parisian boudoir, 80, 82, *82*
piped lampshades, 104
punched tin lantern, 106
striped and beaded lampshades, 104
Swedish bedroom, 68
lined curtains, 121
linen-covered settee, 127
lino tiles, 39
loft, New York, 38-43, *38-43*
Long Island look, 10-15, *10-15*
living room, Chinese, 18-23, *18-23*

M
maltese cross, 119
matting, coir, 72
metal fruit bowl, *62*, 115
Mexican look, 56-63, *56-63*
Mexican wall finish, 94
minimalism, 36, 85
mirrors:
Aegean washroom, *88*
Parisian boudoir, *80*, 82
pewter-covered mirror frame, 111

silvered mirror frame 111
Moroccan look, 30-37, *30-37*
mosaic:
Aegean washroom, 86, *88*, *89*
mosaic-effect wall, 97
mosaic splashback, 98
muslin:
bed canopy, *75*, 129
blinds, *20*, 21

N
New York loft look, 36-43, *36-43*
niches, display, *73*, 76, 112

O
overmantel, ebonized, 135

P
paint effects:
aged plaster wall finish, 93
aqua pigment paint, 58
Mexican wall finish, 94
parchment-effect wall finish, 93
textured wall finish, 94
trompe-l'oeil, 96
woodwashed surface, 95
paper:
découpage screen, *19*, 103
lanterns, *34*, 35
woven paper bowl, *62*, 115
papier mâché, 26
parchment-effect wall finish, 93
parchment lampshade, 107
Parisian boudoir, 78-83, *78-83*
parlour, Georgian, 46-9, *46-9*
patched silk cushions, 118
pedestals, column, 114
pelmets, 123
antiqued pelmet, 142
trellis pelmet, 141
pewter-covered mirror frame, 111

photocopies:
découpage screen, 103
prints, 49
photographs, *39*, 43
picture bows, *68*, 108
pine plate shelf, 133
piped lampshades, 104
plaster:
aged plaster wall finish, 93
Italian look, 26, 28, *29*
plate shelves, *12*, 13, 133
Pompeii, 26
pouffes, 76, *76*
stamped leather pouffe, 127
printed tablecloth, 108
prints, 49
hand-tinted and aged prints, 101
Swedish bedroom, 68
punched tin lantern, 106

R
rattan, 20, *20*
Rhodes, 89
room dividers, New York loft look, 39, *40-41*, 43
'rugs', painted, 46, *48*

S
St John cross, *87*, 89, 110
saris:
bed throws, *74*, 131
curtains, 72-4, *72*, 125
tasselled sari cushions, 117
scaffolding bedhead, 138
Scandinavian look, 64-9, *64-9*
sconces, candle, 76, *76*, 105
Scottish look, 50-55, *50-55*
screens:
Aegean washroom, 86, *86*
alcove screens, 140
bamboo screen, 143
canvas screen, 143
Chinese look, *19*, 20 21, *92*
découpage, 103
fabric-covered metal

screen, 129
glass brick screens, 145
Italian look, 27
New York loft look, *39*, *40-41*, 43
Scottish look, 53-4, *53*, 55
Swedish bedroom, 66, 67
tweed-covered screen, 128
settee, linen-covered, 28-9, 127
shells, 13, *13*, 14, 114
shelving:
Aegean washroom, 86, *87*
alcove shelves, 134
plate shelves, *12*, 13, 133
Mexican look, *61*, 62, 63
wavy shelves, 133
shutters, 61, *62*, 141
silhouettes, *46*, 49, 101
silk:
Chinese look, *20*, 21
patched silk cushions, 118
saris, 72-4, *72*
silvered frame, 111
sink unit doors, *88*, 140
splashback, mosaic, 98
sporting prints, 13
stamped leather pouffe, 127
stamped voile curtains, 121
standard lamps, 21, *23*
stencilling, 95
Aegean washroom, *87*, 89
friezes, *66*, 67, 96
Georgian parlour, 46
Moroccan look, 32
mosaic-effect wall, 97
Scottish look, 53, *54*
storage:
Aegean washroom, 86, *87*
alcove shelves, 134
CD pillars, 28, *28*, 147
Chinese look, 20-21, *21*
customized cube unit, 134
Italian look, 28, *28*
Moroccan look, 32-5, *35*
Parisian boudoir, 81,

83
pine plate shelf, *12*, 13, 133
wavy shelves, 133
striped and beaded lampshades, 104
study, Scottish, 52-5, *52-5*
Swedish bedroom, 65-9, *66-9*

T
tablecloths, printed, *47*, 48-9, *49*, 108
tables:
bamboo tables, 137
Chinese look, *18*, 21
chrome-effect cafe table, 112
Italian look, 26, *26*
Mexican look, *60*
Moroccan look, *32*, 35, *35*
New York loft look, *38*
Parisian boudoir, 81, 82, *82*
small hexagonal table, 136
table on castors, 137
wooden tabletop, 135
tabs, curtains with, 123
tailor's dummy, 81, *83*
tartan, 50, *53*
tasselled sari cushions, 117
templates, 150-55
tented ceilings, *34*, 146
terracotta urn, 113
tesserae, mosaic splashback, 98
textured wall finish, 94
throws:
Italian look, *26*
sari bed throws, *74*, 74, *77*, 131
Scottish look, *53*
tie blinds, 122
tiles, aluminium, 58-61, *58*, 99
tin lanterns, *86*, 89, 106
trays, butler's, 54, *54*
trellis-effect doors, 147
trellis pelmet, 141
trompe-l'oeil, 96
arch, 98
Italian look, 26, *26*, *27*, 28
Scottish look, 53
Tuscan day room, 24-9, *24-9*
tweed, 50, 54

tweed-covered screen, 128

U
uplighters, 28
urns:
terracotta-effect urn, 113
urn firescreen, *27*, 28, 113

V
vases, Parisian boudoir, *80*
voile:
curtains, 81, 121
cushion with voile pockets, 120

W
wall-hanging, appliqué, *53*, 54, 130
walls:
aged plaster wall finish, 93
Mexican wall finish, 94
parchment-effect wall finish, 93
stencilled mosaic-effect wall, 97
textured wall finish, 94
wardrobes, Parisian boudoir, 81, *82*
washroom, Aegean, 84-9, *86-9*
washstands, Swedish bedroom, *66*, 67
wavy shelves, 133
wax, antiquing, 20
wood:
driftwood, *14*
floors, 13
shutters, 141
wooden tabletop, 135
woodwashed surface, 95
worktops, Mexican look, *58*, 61
woven paper bowl, *62*, 115
wrought iron, Italian look, 26, *26*

Z
zinc bath panel, 89, *89*, 102

author's acknowledgments

Special thanks go to Kasha Harmer Hirst for creating the New York loft look.

My love and thanks go to Mark Thurgood, designer and 3D illustrator, without whom this book would never have happened. His dedication and expertise made sure that all my designs not only worked but looked stunning too. My thanks also go to the team who were amazing throughout: Peter Beech, Rita Bonfim, Souki Hildreth, Kevin Hobson, Paul Hughes, Gary Ridgewell and Lynette Smart. Thank you also to all those who put so much effort into their specialist fields: Sally Macloughlan (soft furnishings), Anne Bruce and Chris of Croydon (upholstery), Rosina Lytton Cobbold (murals), Gail Gill (glass), Petra Boase (appliqué) and Terry and Ron from TVS Framing (framing). Also thanks to Rishi, Dominick and Nicki and Ray Munn Ltd for all their help and advice, and to Jenny, Trevor and Jules, Chloe and Paul, and Colin and Kelly for bravely allowing us to transform their rooms and for putting up with the invasions!

My gratitude also goes to Jane O'Shea at Quadrille whose kindness and support through some very difficult times was unending and to Mary Evans for making the book look so wonderful, and not forgetting Pauline, Bridget, Helen, Heather and Rachel, who all helped to bring it all together. My appreciation also goes to Richard Foster for his beautiful photographs which brought the rooms to life and to Bruce Anderson for his lovely shots for part two of the book. Also my thanks to Celia Birtwell whose wonderful fabric design was the key to the creation of our French Boudoir, which gives us pleasure each and every morning when we draw the curtains.

publisher's acknowledgments

The publishers would like to thank all the companies (page 156) who supplied equipment and/or props for photography, and the following for permission to reproduce photographs:

10 left Jérôme Darblay; 10 centre Robert Harding Picture Library/© IPC Magazines Ltd/House & Gardens/Tom Leighton; 10 right Robert Harding Picture Library/© GE Magazines Ltd/Inspirations/Lizzie Orme; 16 above Deidi von Schaewen; 16 above centre International Interiors/Paul Ryan/Architects Pierce & Allen; 16 below centre Hémisphères/Bruno Barbier; 16 below Agence Top/Henri-Alain Segalen; 17 Hémisphères/Bruno Barbier; 24 left Hémisphères/Stéphane Frances; 24 centre left Agence Top/Roland Beaufre; 24 centre right Agence Top/Raymond de Seynes; 24 right Ianthe Ruthven; 25 Hémisphères/Betrand Rieger; 30 Marie Claire Maison/A Perigot/J P Billaud; 31 left Arcaid/Richard Bryant; 31 centre Robert Harding Picture Library/Michael Short; 31 right Marie Claire Maison/Gilles de Chabaneix/Catherine Ardouin; 36 above Houses & Interiors/Verne; 36 below left Frank Spooner Pictures/Gamma; 36 below right Image Bank/Patti McConville; 37 Magnum/Eli Reed; 44 Hémisphères/J P Lescourret; 45 left Impact/Christophe Bluntzer; 45 centre Hémisphères/Stéphane Frances; 45 right The Interior Archive/Simon Brown; 50 above The Image Bank/Chris Close; 50 above centre Impact/Mike McQueen; 50 below centre The Glasgow Picture Library/Eric Thornburn; 50 below Scotland in Focus/Penny Davies; 56 Agence Top/F Le Diascorn; 57 centre left Explorer/G Boutin; 57 centre right Agence Top/Roland Beaufre/Isabelle Goldschmidt, Mexico; 57 left Deidi von Schaewen; 57 right Hémisphères/Bertrand Gardel; 64 Arcaid/Richard Bryant; 65 above Arcaid/Richard Bryant; 65 below left The Interior Archive/Simon Upton/designer Sasha Waddell; 65 below right The Interior Archive/Simon Brown/designer Margaret Howell; 70 centre Hémisphères/Patrick Frilet; 70 left Hémisphères/Patrick Frilet; 70 right Deidi von Schaewen; 71 ffotograff/Patricia Aithie; 78 Guy Hervais; 79 centre left Agence Top/Roland Beaufre; 79 centre right Edifice/Lewis; 79 left Explorer/Lescourret; 79 right Agence Top/Roland Beaufre/Myriam Shaeffer, Paris; 84 Britstock-IFA/Steffl; 85 far left Hémisphères/Annette Soumillard; 85 centre left Magnum/Constantine Manos; 85 centre right Explorer/P Wysocki; 85 far right International Interiors/Paul Ryan/designers D & V Tsingaris.